A Brief History of the Cold War

A BRIEF
HISTORY
OF THE
COLD WAR

LEE EDWARDS & ELIZABETH EDWARDS SPALDING

REGNERY
HISTORY

An earlier edition of this book was published by The Heritage Foundation in 2014 as part of their First Principles Series, ISBN 978-0-89195-152-0

Regnery History™ is a trademark of Salem Communications Holding Corporation; Regnery® is a registered trademark of Salem Communications Holding Corporation

Cataloging-in-Publication data on file with the Library of Congress

ISBN 978-1-62157-486-6

Published in the United States by
Regnery History
An imprint of Regnery Publishing
A Division of Salem Media Group
300 New Jersey Ave NW
Washington, DC 20001
www.RegneryHistory.com

Manufactured in the United States of America

10 9 8 7 6 5 4 3 2 1

Books are available in quantity for promotional or premium use. For information on discounts and terms, please visit our website: www.Regnery.com.

Distributed to the trade by
Perseus Distribution
250 West 57th Street
New York, NY 10107

For Anne and Matthew, our better halves

CONTENTS

ACKNOWLEDGMENTS   ix

INTRODUCTION   1

ONE
THE ORIGINS OF THE COLD WAR (1917–1945)   5

TWO
CONTAINMENT AND THE SOVIET EXPANSION (1945–1950)   23

THREE
THE HOT WARS OF THE COLD WAR (1950–1973)   65

FOUR
DÉTENTE (1969–1980)   107

FIVE
WINNING THE COLD WAR (1981–1991)   141

CONCLUSION
LESSONS FROM THE COLD WAR   191

COLD WAR TIMELINE   201

FOR FURTHER READING AND VIEWING   225

NOTES   235

INDEX   249

ACKNOWLEDGMENTS

We wrote this book because we were not satisfied with the texts we have used in our world history, international relations, and U.S. foreign policy courses. We felt there was a place in the literature for a brief and balanced history of the Cold War. We believe we have succeeded in writing such a book with *A Brief History of the Cold War,* and we invite your comments.

We thank The Heritage Foundation for publishing an early monograph edition of our history. We wish to acknowledge in particular the contribution of Dr. David Azerrad, director of the B. Kenneth Simon Center for Principles and Politics at Heritage, whose skillful editing made this a far better history. We also thank Heritage for its research assistance in the person of the following interns: Josiah Lippencott, Isabel Nelson, and Cooper Nye.

At Regnery History, our editor Tom Spence constantly provided wise suggestions while his colleague Maria Ruhl kept us on schedule. Rarely have we worked with a more professional team.

As always, we count our blessings, especially our spouses, Anne Edwards and Matthew Spalding, without whose love and support we would be lost.

INTRODUCTION

The Cold War was the most protracted and unconventional conflict of the twentieth century. World War I and World War II were great sweeping wars that shaped our history and our world, but they did not match the length or the complexity of the ideological and strategic struggle that occupied superpowers and lesser powers on every continent for more than four decades.

The Cold War was waged on many fronts—from the United States to the Soviet Union, from Europe to Asia, from Africa to Latin America—and by many different kinds of governments: liberal democracies, totalitarian regimes, and everything in between. There were grand

1

strategy and petty politics, shrewd diplomacy and brutal coups. There were elements of economics, religion, and culture. There were shooting wars in Korea and Vietnam, and there were purges, deportations, gulags, and forced famines that killed millions of men, women, and children.

At stake in the Cold War was whether the postwar world would be dominated by the forces of totalitarianism led by the Soviet Union or inspired by the principles of political and economic freedom embodied in the United States. If the expansionist ambitions of the Soviet Union had not been contained, much of Western Europe as well as Eastern Europe might have become communist or at least friendly to communism, isolating the United States strategically and economically for years and perhaps decades to come. Considering that China too was under communist rule, the United States would then have faced powerful, unfriendly regimes to the east and to the west.

When the Second World War ended, the American people sought a return to normalcy, to a concentration on domestic not foreign affairs. Most hoped and expected they could turn over most of the responsibility for international affairs to America's wartime allies—Great Britain and Soviet Russia—and to the United Nations.

But six debilitating years of war had reduced Britain to a shadow of itself, and a militant Soviet Union, led by Joseph Stalin, was determined to proceed with its grand design of socializing the world. As for the UN, it was a new and untested organization. Quite suddenly, there was no one to protect America and its global interests but America itself.

For the next four decades and under nine administrations, Democratic as well as Republican, the United States pursued first a policy of containing the Soviet Union and communism, then a policy of détente and accommodation, and finally a policy of undermining and bringing down what President Ronald Reagan called an "evil empire."

Today's world would be a far different place if the United States had not waged and won—at the cost of tens of thousands of lives and many billions of dollars— the Cold War. That conflict established America as *the* leader of the free world and a global superpower, thereby shaping U.S. diplomacy, military strategy, economic policy, and domestic politics from President Harry Truman to the present.

ONE

THE ORIGINS OF
THE COLD WAR
(1917–1945)

America and Russia, wrote Alexis de Tocqueville, seem called "by some secret design of Providence" each to hold in its hands "the destinies of half the world." One regime is based on the principles of liberty, equality, the consent of the governed, and the rule of law; the other is grounded in autocracy, tyranny, and servitude. To attain his goal, the American relies on "personal interest and allows the force and the reason of individuals to act, without directing them." The Russian, in contrast, "concentrates all the power of society in one man."[1]

So it appeared to the great French political philosopher in the 1830s when he wrote *Democracy in America*, a work that a century and a half later seemed uncannily prescient as the United States and the Soviet Union waged a forty-five-year conflict over the destiny of the whole world.

The origins of the Cold War, which began in early 1945 with the Yalta summit and ended on Christmas Day 1991 with the dissolution of the Soviet Union, can be traced to the Bolshevik Revolution of 1917, led by Vladimir Lenin, and the birth of the first communist state, the Union of Soviet Socialist Republics (USSR), which adhered to a revolutionary, expansionist ideology.

THE COMMUNIST IDEOLOGY

"The theory of the Communists may be summed up in the single sentence: Abolition of private property."[2] Thus wrote Karl Marx in *The Communist Manifesto*, published in 1848, laying out the doctrine that the abolition of property is a prerequisite to genuine freedom because it prevents the capitalist employer from exploiting the proletarian worker. Marx knew that depriving individual persons of this basic freedom would not be easy and could not "be effected except by means of despotic inroads," that is, dictatorship.[3] To achieve this goal, government must control the means of production, credit and banking systems, and communications and transportation systems. Assuring the proletariat that they had nothing but their chains to lose and a world to win, Marx closed his manifesto with a famous call to arms: "Workers of the world, unite!"[4] Relying on his doctrine of "scientific socialism" (communists use the terms "communist" and "socialist" interchangeably, partially to disguise their objective), which holds that a society without private property is not only desirable but inevitable, Marx's followers would pursue the goal of a global revolution, confident in the eventual liberation of man. But Marx did not foresee the emergence of a prosperous and burgeoning middle class, the foundation of which is private property. As Richard Pipes writes, "Marxism was...dogma masquerading as science."[5]

EARLY EXPANSION

In early 1917, the Tsarist regime that had ruled Russia for more than five hundred years abruptly collapsed, an unexpected casualty of World War I. Led by Lenin, the Bolsheviks took advantage of a political vacuum and by the end of the year seized power. They initiated a campaign of terror that silenced any opposition but controlled only central Russia. The borderlands, inhabited by other nationalities and religions, proclaimed their independence. The Bolshevik response, Pipes writes, was to "conquer by force of arms the lands and peoples that constituted four-fifths of Russia's population." Thus was born the Union of Soviet Socialist Republics that would eventually comprise fifteen countries: Byelorussia, Ukraine, and Moldavia in Eastern Europe; Georgia, Armenia, and Azerbaijan in the Caucasus; Uzbekistan, Turkmenistan, Kazakhstan, Kirghizstan, and Tajikistan in Central Asia; the Baltic states of Estonia, Latvia, and Lithuania; and Russia itself.

In keeping with Marxist-Leninist theory, the Bolsheviks initiated armed conflict first in Russia, then in Europe and the rest of the world. In 1920, Lenin declared that "we knew [in October 1917] that our victory would be a lasting victory only when our undertaking should conquer the whole world."[6] A primary target was the United States—democratic, capitalist, and powerful. Lenin was the first head of state to treat politics, domestic as well as foreign, as warfare, seeking not only to compel "the enemy to submit but to annihilate him."[7] Even during the Russian civil war, the Bolsheviks set into motion plans to communize the world.

The international communist movement was officially launched in March 1919 at the first congress of the Communist International, also known as the Comintern, with representatives from thirty countries, including the United States, Russia, Germany, France, Great Britain, China, Korea, Hungary, Poland, Finland, the three Baltic countries, Sweden, and Persia. The various communist parties were not independent entities but national sections of the Comintern, which controlled and monitored their activities. The Comintern's newspaper, the *Communist International*, provided the party line for every national organization. Grigorii Zinoviev, the head of the Communist International, boasted, "The movement advances with such dizzying speed that one can confidently say...in a year all Europe shall be Communist. And the struggle for Communism shall be transferred to America, and perhaps also to Asia and other parts of the world."[8]

Trying to take advantage of the chaotic state of Europe and the Middle East following World War I, the Soviets staged a failed revolution in Germany and attempted, unsuccessfully, to establish a communist regime in Persia (present-day Iran). In the summer of 1920, they invaded Poland, seeking to use it as a communist base to conquer

Western Europe. They were repelled by the Polish army, forcing the Soviets to conclude that they did not yet have sufficient power to export revolution beyond their borders, but they continued to plant seeds of revolution and foster acts of espionage around the world.

The fifth congress of the Comintern, held in 1924, called for the overthrow of non-communist regimes and their control by Moscow. By then there were thirty-seven communist parties in nations as far removed from the borders of the Soviet Union as the United States and Chile. Estonia's communist party staged a coup that failed. Severe economic problems inside the Soviet Union hampered but did not halt international subversive activities.

At the seventh congress of the Communist International, held in Moscow in 1935, the new Comintern leader, Georgi Dimitrov, called for a Popular Front against fascism. Communist parties, which had been denouncing liberals and socialists, now urged an alliance with them to stop the spread of fascism in Italy and Germany.[9]

STALIN AND THE GREAT TERROR

Joseph Stalin succeeded Lenin as the leader of the Soviet Union in 1924 and ruled with an iron fist for nearly thirty years. He used executions, purges, imprisonment, famine, forced relocation, and other repressive methods to stay in power. "Death solves all problems," Stalin is alleged to have said. "No man, no problem." An estimated seven million persons died in the forced famine in Ukraine (the Holodomor). The Great Terror of 1936–1938, a campaign of sham trials and executions, took nearly a million lives. Many incriminated themselves to end their ordeal. Millions more—political dissidents and common criminals—perished in the Gulag, a gigantic system of forced labor camps. By late 1938, all opposition, real and imagined, had been silenced, and Stalin turned his attention to international events.

WORLD WAR II

The Molotov-Ribbentrop Non-Aggression Pact of August 1939 prepared the way for World War II and Stalin's first serious attempt at imperial expansion. He calculated that a treaty with Germany would provoke a major European war, a war that he wanted to last as long as possible. Soviet archives have revealed that Stalin planned to dominate Europe with the help of Hitler's war machine and then eliminate Germany "as a rival for total hegemony over the continent."[10]

Two weeks after Germany invaded Poland from the west, the Red Army invaded from the east. In late September Poland surrendered, and the conquerors divided the country between them, the Soviets acquiring slightly more land but less population than the Germans.

At the same time, Soviet troops began occupying the Baltic states of Estonia, Latvia, and Lithuania. When Finland refused to sign a treaty with the Soviet Union, the Red Army invaded on three fronts but met fierce resistance. It was not until March 1940 that the communist forces could claim victory over the Finns.

These militaristic ventures traumatized the foreign members of the Comintern. For six years, they had denounced Hitler, but now they were directed to oppose the anti-Nazi campaign and condemn Anglo-French "imperialism." Some communists, such as the American spy Whittaker Chambers, rejected Moscow's imperial commands and left the party, but most stayed, still enthralled by the chimera of Marxism-Leninism.

Stalin's first objective following the pact with Germany was to eliminate any opposition in the new territories of the Soviet empire. Orders went out calling for the liquidation of all Nationalists, Trotskyites, and Christian and Social Democrats in the Baltic states. The most notorious of the ensuing atrocities was the execution in April 1940 of some twenty-two thousand Polish prisoners—officers, civil servants, landowners, priests, and policemen. As Brian Crozier writes, they were "lined up, made to dig their own mass graves and shot in the back of the neck." They were buried in the Katyn Forest and other locations in Ukraine and Byelorussia. Official records reveal that the executions were ordered personally by Stalin in a memorandum to the NKVD, the Soviet secret police (later the KGB).[11]

In 1943, Nazi troops discovered some four thousand of the Polish corpses in the Katyn Forest and immediately broadcast the discovery abroad, aiming to embarrass not only Stalin but his wartime allies. Almost everyone in the West dismissed the news as Nazi propaganda, and the truth about the Katyn massacre was not known until Russian President Boris Yeltsin released secret documents from the Kremlin archives in the early 1990s.

While Stalin was annexing half of Poland and incorporating the three Baltic countries into the Soviet Union, public sentiment in the United States had become, if not isolationist, increasingly against involvement in another European war. Throughout the 1930s, the majority of the U.S. public was of the opinion, as the historian Samuel

Eliot Morison put it, that if Europe was stupid enough to start another war, "America should resolutely stay out."[12]

President Franklin Roosevelt didn't even mention foreign policy in his second inaugural address in 1937. His only significant initiative regarding the Soviet Union had come early in 1933, when he extended formal diplomatic recognition to Moscow. Expecting increased U.S.-Soviet trade, the administration had extracted a promise from the Soviet foreign minister, Maxim Litvinov, that his country would end communist activity in the United States, guarantee religious freedom in the USSR, and negotiate a settlement of claims and debts. Stalin ignored Litvinov's promises and stepped up Soviet spying in America. The expected trade never materialized.

American policy makers were essentially indifferent to Soviet affairs. In the fall of 1939, Whittaker Chambers informed Assistant Secretary of State A. A. Berle, the president's intelligence liaison, that for most of the decade he had been a member of a Soviet espionage ring in Washington that included a State Department official named Alger Hiss. Berle was not moved to take any immediate action, noting in his diary that he had met anti-communists before who tended to exaggerate their experiences.[13]

By late 1939, strict American neutrality had become untenable. President Roosevelt persuaded Congress to amend neutrality legislation so that belligerents, including Great Britain, could obtain U.S. war materiel on a pay-on-delivery basis. The new policy did not deter Hitler. In April 1940 Nazi forces swept through Denmark and Norway and then swung south toward France, a dramatic advance that was possible because they did not have to contend with a Russian army.

Congress responded in June with a four-billion-dollar appropriation for a "two-ocean navy" and, three months later, the first peacetime conscription in American history. In March 1941, following Roosevelt's historic reelection to a third term as president, Congress approved the Lend-Lease Act, permitting the president to sell, lease, or lend defense articles to any country deemed vital to U.S. defense.

In late June, Hitler invaded Russia, turning the USSR into an American ally. Roosevelt immediately extended lend-lease terms to the Soviets, and the United States provided substantial aid to them in the months before Pearl Harbor and afterward. Hitler had committed the greatest part of the German army—between 125 and two hundred divisions—to defeating the Soviets, and the effort to liberate France would depend on keeping the Germans tied down on the Eastern front.

To attract Western support for its fight against Hitler, Moscow dissolved the Comintern in 1943, a gesture suggesting that it had abandoned its goal of world revolution. Stalin assured the Allies that he sought only "Socialism in one country,"[14] one of his characteristic lies in pursuit of an immediate political goal and consistent with communist ideology.

YALTA

In the closing months of the war, as Germany's defenses crumbled, the Red Army advanced on a thousand-mile-wide front, taking Warsaw, pushing into Germany from the north and the south, moving into Hungary and Czechoslovakia, and threatening Vienna. The Soviet advance gave Moscow a tremendous bargaining advantage when Stalin met with Roosevelt and British Prime Minister Winston Churchill at Yalta in the Crimean peninsula in early 1945 to discuss such crucial issues as the future of Europe and the war in the Pacific.

The Japanese had vowed to defend their country to the last soldier, and the atomic bomb was yet to be tested. The Soviet Union had so far remained neutral in the war against Japan, and Roosevelt—along with his chiefs of staff—was convinced that Japan could be defeated only with Soviet help. Churchill wanted to restrict the expansion of Soviet power in Europe, while Stalin wanted to extend Soviet influence as far westward as possible. While desiring a democratic Europe, Roosevelt's attention was focused on the Pacific. As they considered the composition of post-war Europe, Roosevelt and Churchill based their proposals on the expectation that communists and non-communists in a liberated country such as Poland or Czechoslovakia could form a regime like the "popular front" governments in Europe before the war. Such a balance of disparate interests would require the full cooperation of the Soviet Union, which Roosevelt and Churchill expected would be forthcoming.

On the surface, it seemed that the Americans and the British got what they wanted at Yalta. The Soviets agreed to enter the war against Japan within three months after Germany's surrender. Stalin knew he was joining a war that would require a minimal military commitment yet allow him to share in the spoils of victory. He also agreed to compromise on questions of membership in a new international organization, the United Nations, on which Roosevelt placed high hopes.

The negotiators at Yalta agreed to divide Germany into four occupation zones—one each for the United States, Great Britain, the Soviet Union, and France. This arrangement pleased Churchill, eager for France's restoration as an important power in Europe and opposed to any Soviet control of Germany. Regarding Poland, the three leaders established a temporary Polish-Soviet border, the Curzon Line, with Poles on one side and Byelorussians and Ukrainians on the other.

But on the issue of who would govern Poland, Stalin refused to recognize the non-communist government in exile that had been operating from London for six years, recognizing instead the government the Soviets had set up in Lublin. Roosevelt and Churchill accepted ambiguous language about the make-up of a future Polish government and Stalin's promise of "free and unfettered elections in the near future," an agreement that Roosevelt's chief of staff, Admiral William D. Leahy, dismissed as "so elastic that the Russians can stretch it all the way from Yalta to Washington without breaking it."[15]

Stalin also agreed to establish interim governments, "broadly representative of all democratic elements," in the rest of liberated Europe—Austria, Hungary, Czechoslovakia, Bulgaria, and Romania—to be followed by "free" elections. The agreement was part of a grandiose "Declaration on Liberated Europe," drafted by the Americans, which the Soviet leader was quite content to sign after Roosevelt announced that all American forces would leave Europe within two years.[16]

By late March 1945, Churchill was writing to Roosevelt that nearly everything they had agreed to at Yalta was unraveling, while the president (who had reassured those around him that he could handle Stalin) was having second thoughts about the Soviet leader. Informed that the elections in Eastern Europe would be held Soviet style, he exploded, "Averell [Harriman] is right. We can't do business with Stalin. He has broken every one of the promises he made at Yalta."[17] Nevertheless, FDR's messages to Churchill for the rest of March and into April were intended to placate the prime minister. He did not want the United States and Great Britain to be seen as opposing Stalin, whose commitment to the war in the South Pacific he and his military advisers considered essential. In his final cable to Churchill, Roosevelt said, "I would minimize the general Soviet problem as much as possible because these problems, in one form or another, seem to arise every day and most of them straighten out as in the case of the Bern meeting," concluding, "We must be firm, however, and our course thus far is correct."[18] Roosevelt's firmness differed in kind from Churchill's but not in intent. On April 12, the president died of a cerebral hemorrhage and the conduct of U.S. foreign policy abruptly shifted to his vice president of just three months, Harry S. Truman.

CHINA

Beginning in the 1920s, China suffered through a long and brutal civil war between the Red Army of Mao Zedong and the Nationalist forces of Chiang Kai-shek. Having gained the upper hand by the 1930s, Chiang instituted a promising program of reconstruction and economic development for the new Republic of China. Mao, seemingly no longer a factor in Chinese affairs, was holed up in the northern province of Shensi. But when the Japanese invaded China in 1937, Chiang and Mao were obliged, reluctantly, to join forces against a common enemy.

For the next eight years, the Nationalists bore the brunt of the fighting—tying up as many as one million Japanese troops—while the communists fought only when they had the chance to take on a much smaller enemy. Mao's strategy was revealed in a secret directive published a decade later: "The Sino-Japanese war affords our party an excellent opportunity for expansion. Our policy should be 70 percent expansion, 20 percent dealing with the [Nationalists], and 10 percent resisting Japan."[19]

With the surrender of Japan in August 1945, the communists resumed China's dormant civil war. At first, it was official U.S. policy to support the Nationalists, but American diplomats in China began promoting a united front of Nationalists and communists, reassuring Washington that Mao and his colleagues were simply "agrarian reformers."[20] At this critical point, the Soviet Union handed over to the Chinese communists a massive supply of arms and military equipment seized from Japanese forces when it took control of Manchuria. In contrast and in an effort to bring about a coalition government, Washington imposed an embargo on American arms to the Nationalists. When Chiang refused to join with the Chinese communists, a frustrated President Truman announced a hands-off policy on China, contributing to an inevitable Nationalist defeat.

Throughout 1947–1948, city after city fell to the communists, until on October 1, 1949, Mao Zedong declared the formation of the People's Republic of China. Chiang Kai-shek had already left the mainland to establish a government in exile on Taiwan. The U.S. State Department denied any responsibility for the "loss of China," which would become a major issue in the 1952 presidential campaign. Congressman Walter Judd, a leading expert on U.S. foreign policy, disagreed with State's disclaimer, pointing out that the United States, having promised Manchuria to Nationalist China, contributed decisively to China's turning communist by handing Manchuria over to the Soviets at Yalta. The 1946–1947 arms embargo, moreover, had deprived the Nationalists of ammunition at a crucial point in the civil war. "Communist conquest of China," Judd warned, "is a mortal peril to all Asia."[21] Judd's words proved prophetic when China played a key role in the Korean War and later in the fall of Indochina to communism.

Stalin was well satisfied with the outcome in China, and Mao Zedong acknowledged him as the leader of the worldwide communist revolution.

TWO

CONTAINMENT AND THE SOVIET EXPANSION
(1945–1950)

The need for a policy of containment emerged almost immediately after victory was declared in Europe in April 1945. Soviet troops remained in place throughout Central and Eastern Europe, as Stalin stressed the need for "friendly" nations next to Russia. In a "Long Telegram" sent from Moscow in late February 1946, George Kennan explained to his State Department colleagues in Washington that all Soviet efforts on the international plane were bound to be inimical to the United States and the West. Soviet power, however, "is highly sensitive to the logic [of] force" and usually withdraws "when strong resistance is encountered."[1] President

Harry Truman, who had already declared in a memorandum that he was tired of always accommodating the Soviets, was ahead of Kennan and would chart a firm U.S. policy with the Truman Doctrine, the Marshall Plan, and the North Atlantic Treaty Organization (NATO). The Long Telegram arrived at the right time in Washington but did not form the foundation for everything that followed.

HARRY TRUMAN: THE FIRST COLD WARRIOR

Though often depicted as a nonentity in foreign policy, Truman, who had served in France during World War I, had considerable experience as a U.S. senator and was an astute student of world history. The man from Missouri knew farming and small business, and he held strong political and religious convictions. On the former, he was both Democratic and democratic; on the latter, he was ecumenical, although he believed that his Baptist faith gave man the most direct route to God. No fuzzy idealist, he advocated the use of strength if required to achieve or sustain world peace. As long as fallible men ran the world, he reasoned, strength was needed to defend the cause of freedom.

Throughout April and May 1945—especially before V-E Day on May 9, when World War II officially ended new British prime minister, Clement Atlee, who had replaced Churchill after a general election earlier that month, objected to Soviet policies in Poland and the attempts to control the Black Sea straits. Truman left Potsdam, his first summit, convinced of Stalin's consuming desire for political power, putting the new president at some distance from FDR.

Roosevelt had expected the postwar world to be characterized by spheres of influence and a balance of power maintained by what he called the "Four Policemen"—the United States, Great Britain, the Soviet Union, and China. In such an arrangement, he believed, the USSR would feel secure and act like a traditional great power. But almost from the beginning of his presidency, Truman was skeptical about FDR's interpretation of world politics and the Soviet Union, and he soon committed himself and the United States to a policy of firmness toward the Kremlin. In a late April conversation with Secretary of State Edward Stettinius and Averell Harriman, the ambassador to the Soviet Union, Truman emphasized that he would tell the visiting Soviet foreign minister, Vyacheslav Molotov, "in words of one syllable" that the Polish question must be settled in accord with the Yalta agreements, that is, with free and open elections.[2]

in Europe—Truman cabled back and forth with Sta
and Churchill in an attempt to prevent the USSR fro
acquiring more territory. Churchill wanted the dem
cratic allies to change course regarding the Soviet Uni
but Truman felt obliged to honor the agreement FDR I
made at Yalta.

Furthermore, American soldiers were war-we
and didn't relish another conflict in Europe, especi
against the Soviet Union, a former ally. The war in
Pacific also required additional U.S. troops. Trun
could only hope that the Soviets would honor their Y
promises.

At the Potsdam conference in late July, the presic
confirmed the Soviets' intention to enter the war aga
Japan which, however, they did not do until Augus
two days after the United States dropped the ato
bomb on Hiroshima. Truman informed Stalin at P
dam that America had a new weapon of enorm
power. Stalin displayed little interest because he alre
knew about the building of the bomb through the
of Soviet spies in the United States.

The conferees agreed on little beyond the four-pc
occupation of Germany. The Soviets' demand for
billion in reparations was turned down. Truman and

What emerges from the private and public record of the first few months of the new American administration is that Truman, though he did not want to alienate the USSR, was concerned about the Kremlin's aggressive foreign policy. He hoped to avoid any appearance of the United States' and Great Britain's "ganging up" on the Soviet Union but recognized the serious philosophical differences between communism and democracy. "I've no faith in any Totalitarian State," he noted. All these states, he said, "start with a wrong premise—that lies are justified and that the old disproven Jesuit formula— the end justifies the means is right and necessary to maintain the power of government."[3]

Truman made no direct mention of the Soviet Union in his State of the Union address in January 1946, but earlier that month he had revealed his ideas about the East-West conflict and his early thoughts about containment in a forceful memorandum. The president expressed his anger over the Soviets' actions before, during, and after Potsdam as well as their designs on the Baltic states. He urged all possible vigor against the "Russian program" in Iran, where "now Russia stirs up rebellion and keeps troops." Connecting Soviet conduct in Iran to its larger ambitions in the Middle East, Truman wrote that there was not "a doubt in my mind that Russia intends an invasion of Turkey and the seizure of the Black Sea Straits to the Mediterranean." Unless the Soviet Union was faced with "an iron fist and strong language another war is in the making." Force was all it responded to, Truman asserted, usually asking—"How many divisions have you?" After listing a number of areas critical to U.S. interests, from the Black Sea Straits to China and Korea, the president bluntly concluded his memorandum, "I'm tired of babying the Soviets."[4]

But Truman was circumscribed in his actions by the mood of the American people and the reduced state of American forces. With the unconditional surrender of Japan, Americans sought a return to normalcy and a concentration on domestic rather than foreign affairs. After all, they reasoned, the United States had won the war, defeated both the Germans and the Japanese, and hosted the founding of the United Nations. Surely the future of Europe could be placed in the hands of our wartime allies, Britain and the Soviet Union, and the newly formed United Nations.

A massive demobilization ensued. In May 1945, at the end of the European conflict, the United States had an army of 3.5 million men in Europe. By March 1946, there were only four hundred thousand troops left, mainly new recruits. The air force and the navy carried out similar across-the-board reductions.

But while the nation was demobilizing and Congress was debating the extension of wage and price controls, the USSR was preparing for conflict. In a formal election address in February 1946, Stalin blamed World War II on "monopoly capitalism" and warned that future conflicts were inevitable because of the "present capitalist development of [the] world economy." He called on the Soviet people to develop heavy industry "and all kinds of scientific research"—that is, military research—for the next fifteen years if necessary. "Only under such conditions," Stalin declared ominously, "will our country be insured against any eventuality."[5]

His belligerence disturbed many in Washington, including Justice William O. Douglas of the Supreme Court, who suggested that Stalin's speech meant "the declaration of World War III." *Newsweek* referred to the address as the "most war-like pronouncement uttered by any statesman since V-J Day."[6]

THE IRON CURTAIN DESCENDS

Rarely does an out-of-office politician have a major impact on public policy, especially outside his own country, but Winston Churchill was no ordinary politician. As a personal favor to Truman, he traveled to the president's home state in March 1946 to deliver a speech at Westminster College. While the two men traveled together by train, Truman read Churchill's text, remarking that "it was admirable and would do nothing but good, although it would make quite a stir."[7] Churchill was about to make one of the most memorable speeches of the Cold War.

"From Stettin in the Baltic to Trieste in the Adriatic," Churchill began, "an Iron Curtain has descended across the Continent. Behind that line lie all the capitals of the ancient states of central and eastern Europe." All these cities and the populations around them, he said, lie in "what I might call the Soviet sphere, and are all subject, in one form or another, not only to Soviet influence but to a very high and in many cases increasing measure of control from Moscow."[8]

To stop Soviet expansionism, Churchill called for a "fraternal association of the English-speaking peoples," military as well as economic in nature. Such an alliance, he believed, would decrease the risk of war rather than the opposite: "From what I have seen of our Russian friends and allies during the war, I am convinced that there is nothing they admire so much as strength, and there is nothing for which they have less respect than for weakness, especially military weakness."[9]

Churchill made two other points critical to an understanding of American and Western conduct in the Cold War. He cited Soviet subversion and espionage in noncommunist nations around the world, and he warned that the bitter experience of Munich would be repeated unless firm action was taken. While others avoided publicly calling the Soviet Union a tyranny, Churchill specified the aims and actions of the Soviet regime as fundamental impediments to building as well as sustaining the sinews of peace.[10]

Stung by Churchill's remarks, Stalin responded angrily that the British statesman had sounded "a call to war with the Soviet Union." He declared sarcastically that World War II had not been fought "for the sake of exchanging the lordship of Hitler for the lordship of Churchill." Regarding Soviet "dominance" of its neighbors, Stalin said that Soviet security required that neighboring governments be "loyal."[11]

The *New York Times* responded to Stalin's tirade by pointing out that since 1940 the Soviet Union had annexed thirteen nations and territories comprising 273,947 square miles and a population of 24,355,500.

Asked the *Times*, "Where does the search for security end and where does expansion begin?"[12]

Even before Churchill's Iron Curtain speech, Truman decided to test the thesis that the Soviet Union was "highly sensitive to the logic of force." In January 1946, a pro-Soviet government came to power in Iran and began to negotiate with the autonomous region of Azerbaijan in Northern Iran, occupied by Soviet forces. Truman demanded that Stalin withdraw all Soviet soldiers and warned that the American fleet was prepared to move into the area within six weeks. On March 24, Moscow announced that all Soviet troops would be withdrawn from Iran; by the end of May they were gone.

Truman saw Soviet aggression in Iran as part of a pattern of communist behavior and was prepared to take appropriate action against any further communist encroachment. He did not have to wait long.

The Soviets sought throughout 1945 and the first half of the following year to gain control of the Dardanelles, the waterway between the Black Sea and the eastern Mediterranean. In August 1946, Moscow renewed a demand for a new administration of the straits which would have in effect turned Turkey into a Soviet satellite. Truman responded forcefully by dispatching to the region the aircraft carrier *Franklin D. Roosevelt* along with a contingent of Marines. Once again, Stalin backed away, adding more credence to the president's policy of calculated firmness.

It now remained for Truman, in response to continued Soviet aggressiveness, to take specific steps to formulate what became known as the Truman Doctrine—a policy of supporting free peoples who resist "subjugation" from either inside or outside anti-democratic forces.

PRECURSORS TO THE TRUMAN DOCTRINE: THE LONG TELEGRAM AND THE WAR MEMO

In February 1946, George F. Kennan, the U.S. deputy chief of mission in Moscow, sent what came to be called the "Long Telegram" to the State Department in Washington. He had been asked by State why Moscow would not adhere to the rules and regulations of the World Bank and the International Monetary Fund. Frustrated by the apparent unwillingness of official Washington to understand or accept the reality of Soviet aims and actions, Kennan made the inquiry an occasion to give his superiors "the whole truth" about what the Soviet Union was up to as well as its intentions and to suggest a strategy in response.

His analysis identified the following basic Soviet attitudes:

1. The USSR believes that it lives in an antagonistic "capitalist encirclement" with which there can be no permanent peaceful coexistence.
2. The Kremlin is convinced, therefore, that everything possible must be done to advance the relative strength of the Soviet Union.
3. Soviet suspicion of the world is based on the traditional Russian sense of insecurity.
4. The Soviets will seek to undermine the general political and strategic potential of major Western powers.
5. All Soviet efforts on the international scene will be negative and destructive.

"We have here," Kennan wrote, "a political force committed fanatically to the belief that with the U.S. there can be no permanent *modus vivendi*, that it is desirable and necessary that the internal harmony of our society be disrupted, our traditional way of life be destroyed, the international authority of our state be broken, if Soviet power is to be secure."

Nevertheless, said Kennan, Soviet power is "highly sensitive to the logic of force. For this reason it can easily withdraw—and usually does—when strong resistance is encountered at any point. Thus, if the adversary has sufficient force and makes clear his readiness to use it, he rarely has to do so."[13] Kennan did not use the word "containment," but the implications were clear: a policy of patience and firmness with an emphasis on the latter should be pursued. There should be no more concessions to the Soviet Union. Differences should be openly aired but in a non-provocative manner.[14]

Kennan's analysis is a classic statement of balance-of-power politics. While the Long Telegram crystallized the need—ten months into the Truman presidency—for a coherent foreign policy, it did not originate a strategy of containment. Kennan left unaddressed, for example, Soviet military capabilities, which would be one of Truman's central concerns. He also downplayed the weight of ideology in Soviet affairs, another point of difference with the president, although he did call communism a "fanatically" committed political force.

President Truman, on the other hand, while incorporating Russian history into his analysis, emphasized the role of communist ideology in Soviet aggression. Backed by Secretary of the Navy James Forrestal (soon to be the first secretary of defense), Truman looked upon communism as a secular, millennial religion that shaped the Kremlin's worldview and inspired an offensive foreign policy, making the Soviet Union a threat to liberty and peace everywhere.

A few months later, the president asked Clark Clifford, his special counsel, to prepare a memorandum about the agreements that the Soviets had kept and those it had broken. With his aide George M. Elsey, Clifford presented in September 1946 a top-secret report titled "American Relations with the Soviet Union." Echoing the Long Telegram, Clifford and Elsey affirmed that military power "is the only language the disciples of power politics [in Moscow] understand." Going beyond Kennan's analysis, they concluded that the United States "should support and assist all democratic countries in any way menaced or endangered by the USSR"—the first articulation of such a policy—but did not advocate all-out war. While conceding that Soviet leaders believed that conflict between the West and the East was "irreconcilable," Clifford and

Elsey expressed the hope that the Soviets would work toward "a fair and equitable settlement" of differences once they realized that "we are too strong to be beaten and too determined to be frightened."[15]

The main thesis of the Clifford-Elsey memorandum—that the United States should support endangered democratic countries—is threaded through Truman's own words, the administration's actions from 1947 through 1949, and National Security Council documents like the pivotal NSC 68. Clifford and Elsey quoted extensively from the Long Telegram but diverged from it on the subject of Soviet ideology. Kennan maintained that the Soviets engaged in traditional power politics under the guise of Marxism. Clifford and Elsey, by contrast, presented the Soviet Union in 1946 as distinct from Russia and its history, arguing that the Kremlin was "blinded by its adherence to Marxist doctrine."

They took Stalin's election address seriously, incorporated Churchill's observation that the Soviets wanted the fruits of war without war, and recognized that the Soviets believed in the inevitability of conflict between democracy and communism. The final part of the memorandum recommended a new U.S. policy. Though America should recognize that the Soviets' "aggressive militaristic imperialism" jeopardized the world, its primary objective should be to convince the Kremlin that it was in its interest to participate in a system of global cooperation.[16]

At first such a policy appears paradoxical. But Truman's position was that, while the free world was unable to reverse previous Soviet gains, it would refuse to allow additional aggression and expansion of the Soviet empire. Far from seeking some status quo arrangement, the United States would challenge Soviet imperialism in principle and practice.

THE TRUMAN DOCTRINE

The combination of one of the worst winters in history and the economic consequences of World War II reduced Great Britain in early 1947 to near bankruptcy. On February 21, the British Embassy in Washington, D.C., informed the State Department that Britain could no longer play its traditional role of protecting Greece and Turkey against threats external and internal and would have to withdraw from the region by April 1.

Since Greece faced internal agitation by communists and Turkey confronted a hostile Soviet Union, only a firm American commitment could prevent Soviet control of the two strategically located countries. There was no one to protect the strategic interests of the United States but the United States itself. Great Britain's withdrawal from the international stage had left a political vacuum, and the United States moved to fill it, not for narrow commercial or territorial reasons, but to protect freedom, independent states, and allies in a crucial area of the world.

On February 26, Secretary of State George Marshall and Undersecretary of State Dean Acheson brought their recommendations to President Truman. Greece needed substantial aid and quickly; the alternative would be the loss of Greece and the extension of the Iron Curtain across the eastern Mediterranean. Truman wrote in his memoirs, "The ideals and the traditions of our nation demanded that we come to the aid of Greece and Turkey and that we put the world on notice that it would be our policy to support the cause of freedom wherever it was threatened."[17]

Central to the development of the Truman Doctrine was the president's February 27 session with congressional leaders. Republicans controlled both houses of Congress following the mid-term elections, and Truman understood that he needed the help of the Republican leaders to craft a bipartisan foreign policy. At the White House meeting, Truman asked Marshall to summarize the case for Greek and Turkish aid, which the secretary did in his usual matter-of-fact way. There was a tepid response from the congressional group. Understanding what was at stake, Acheson intervened with a dire warning that the Soviets were playing "one of the greatest gambles in history." The United States alone was in a position "to break up the play."[18]

Silence ensued, broken at last by a solemn Senator Arthur Vandenberg, the Republicans' foreign policy leader, who said, "Mr. President, if you will say that to the Congress and the country, I will support you, and I believe that most of its members will do the same."[19]

Truman based the assistance on the belief that governments suited to the peoples of Greece and Turkey would not develop or succeed if tyranny prevailed in those countries. But his concern went farther than the hopes of the Greek and Turkish peoples for a democratic future. He also stressed the implications of communist pressure on the entire region and on the world, asserting that the totalitarian pattern had to be broken.

The consolidation of Soviet power in Eastern Europe depended on the local conditions in each country, the strength of the communist-led wartime resistance movements, and the degree of direct Soviet intervention. The Kremlin had promised in the Paris peace treaties to remove its troops from Bulgaria, Romania, and Hungary but had failed to do so. As a result, the communists were able to force the socialists to join them in coalitions they dominated. Moscow had also manipulated the Polish elections to eliminate Stanisław Mikołajczyk and his Polish Peasant Party, with the help of a hundred thousand Polish security police agents, modeled on the Soviet NKVD.

Because the Red Army did not occupy either Greece or Turkey, Truman saw an opportunity to encourage liberty in the two countries by strengthening domestic conditions and preventing Soviet intervention on behalf of the local communists. He signed the Greek and Turkish aid bill into law on May 22, 1947, declaring, "The conditions of peace include, among other things, the ability of nations to maintain order and independence and to support themselves economically."[20] Although he did not name the Soviet Union, Truman said that totalitarianism was hindering peace and encroaching on peoples' territories and lives and called for an unprecedented American involvement in foreign affairs in peacetime.

The assertion of the Truman Doctrine was truly historic—the first time since the Monroe Doctrine of 1823 that an American president had explicitly defined a principle of foreign policy and put the world on notice.

In the absence of an effective United Nations, the president said, America was the one nation capable of establishing and maintaining peace. The international situation, he said, was at a critical juncture. If America failed to aid Greece and Turkey "in this fateful hour," the crisis would take on global proportions. While political and economic means were preferred, military strength was also needed to foster the political and economic stability of threatened countries.

The Truman Doctrine was a primary building block of containment. The president sounded themes that endured throughout his and successive administrations. The United States, he said, must support free peoples who were resisting attempted subjugation by armed minorities or outside pressures so that free peoples can "work out their own destinies in their own way."[21]

Faced with a war unlike any previous one, Truman laid the groundwork for a policy of peace through strength. Against the backdrop of postwar domestic needs and wants, he had to educate the American people and persuade congressional leaders that decisive U.S. engagement in a new world struggle was necessary. Between 1946 and 1950, he reached three conclusions regarding global politics:

1. Freedom must precede order, for freedom provides the deepest roots for peace. He rejected the realist preference for order above all.
2. What kind of government a people chooses is decisive in both domestic and international politics. He did not echo President Woodrow Wilson's call for self-determination with a secondary concern for governing principles. For Truman, a commitment to justice was the overriding principle.
3. Security and strength go hand in hand. Truman's definition of strength included political order and military muscle, that is, a government and people embracing and then maintaining their liberty and justice.

President Truman and his administration proceeded to build on this political foundation. The impending economic collapse of Britain, France, and most of Western Europe in the winter of 1946 and the spring of 1947 led the United States to take action in the economic sphere in the form of the Marshall Plan. Soviet expansionism, including the establishment of puppet governments in Poland, Bulgaria, Romania, and Czechoslovakia, Communist agitation in Italy and France, and the Berlin blockade spurred the United States and its allies to form NATO, America's first military alliance in peacetime. NSC 68 added an international dimension to the concept of peace through political, economic, and military strength.

"X" AND "THE SOURCES OF SOVIET CONDUCT"

In the summer of 1947, following Congress's adoption of the Truman Doctrine and the effective announcement of the Marshall Plan by Secretary Marshall at Harvard University, the journal *Foreign Affairs* published an article by a mysterious author identified only as "X" and titled "The Sources of Soviet Conduct." "X" was in fact George Kennan, and the article proposed "containment" as the proper U.S. policy toward the Soviet Union.

Kennan argued that Soviet policy was "a fluid stream which moves constantly, wherever it is permitted to move, toward a given goal. Its main concern is to make sure that it has filled every nook and cranny available to it in the basin of world power." However, Kennan said, the Soviets will accommodate themselves to "unassailable barriers," and the United States has the power to "force upon the Kremlin a far greater degree of moderation and circumspection than it has had to observe in recent years." The central method of bringing about this adjustment by the Soviets, he wrote, was "containment":

> [I]t is clear that the main element of any United States policy toward the Soviet Union must be that of ... a long-term vigilant containment of Russian expansive tendencies. ... The Soviet pressure against the free institutions of the Western world is something that can be contained by the adroit and vigilant application of counter-force at a series of constantly shifting geographical and political points, corresponding to the shifts and maneuvers of Soviet policy.[22]

As he always did, Kennan emphasized the psychological over the political. He downgraded the most basic source of Soviet conduct—communism. According to him, circumstances rather than ideology determined Kremlin behavior. The communists established a dictatorship in 1917 out of necessity and not conviction. Kennan interpreted all governing as the exercise of power; dictatorship simply signified that fewer persons held the power. He did not explore either the nature of tyranny and liberty or whether communists' behavior, apart from history and culture, stemmed from their ideology. But as we have seen with the early formation of the Comintern and the post–World War II attempts to bring down the governments of France and Italy, only ideology explains the Soviet Union's decades-long campaign to communize the world. Kennan rejected any such analysis. The central message of the "X" article was that a U.S. policy of patience would permit the insecure leaders of the USSR—in perhaps ten to fifteen years—to mellow and loosen their grip on the Russian people. Although he popularized the term "containment" with the *Foreign Affairs* article, Kennan did not conceive containment as practiced by the Truman administration, including the Marshall Plan and NATO.

THE MARSHALL PLAN

On April 5, 1947, Walter Lippmann, the most influential columnist of the day, wrote that "the danger of a European economic collapse is the threat that hangs over us and all the world." So serious was the situation in France that the State Department unofficially sent John Foster Dulles to assess the possibility of a communist coup or a civil war between the communists—the second-largest political party in France—and the supporters of Charles de Gaulle, the leader of the Free French during World War II. Finding France torn by strikes, sabotage, and political strife, Dulles reported that prompt economic help was essential to the future of a free and secure France.

In London, Winston Churchill described Europe's broken and ravished condition and declared that only in unity could the continent achieve economic well-being and security from aggression. Undersecretary of State Will Clayton, returning home after six weeks in Europe, wrote an urgent memorandum for the president, warning that "without further prompt and substantial aid from the United States, economic, social and political disintegration will overwhelm Europe."[23]

What was needed, all these observers were saying, was not more U.S. relief but a plan to revive agriculture, industry, and trade so that the stricken countries of Western Europe might once again become self-supporting.

It was in this context that Secretary of State Marshall accepted an invitation to speak at Harvard's commencement exercises in June 1947. There he outlined what came to be called the Marshall Plan, one of the three essential elements of containment, along with the Truman Doctrine and the North Atlantic Treaty Organization, which would be established two years later.

The European Recovery Program (ERP) proposed by Marshall was economic in its means but political as to its ends. The ERP's purpose was "the revival of a working economy in the world" so as to permit "the emergence of political and social conditions in which free institutions can exist." As Truman later explained, "the world now realizes that without the Marshall Plan it would have been difficult for Western Europe to remain free from the tyranny of communism."[24]

The United States offered the twelve billion dollars of the plan in the form of grants, not loans, to all of Europe. Stalin quickly rejected the ERP and directed the Soviet satellite countries not to participate, further dividing Europe and setting in motion forces that would create a dangerous bipolar world.

Passage of the ERP in Congress was never in doubt, but passage by a large majority was assured on February 24, 1948, when communists carried out a coup d'état in Czechoslovakia. With the Soviet army poised on the border, communist "action committees" roamed the country, suppressing all political opposition. Klement Gottwalk formed a new cabinet dominated by communists, and the Czechoslovak Republic, which had been a symbol of democracy in Central Europe since the end of World War I, was transformed overnight into a communist satellite. The Czech coup shocked the West from Paris to London to Washington, casting what James Forrestal called a new and frightening light "upon the power, ferocity, and scope of communist aggression."[25]

On April 2, in an act of historic bipartisanship, Congress overwhelmingly passed the European Recovery Program. In little more than a year, the Republican Eightieth Congress had approved the Truman Doctrine, establishing that international peace and U.S. security were intertwined, and the Marshall Plan, committing America to the economic and political well-being of Western Europe. It would next approve the most controversial component of U.S. foreign policy in the postwar period—the Vandenberg Resolution, which prepared the way for NATO.

NATO

In response to the communist takeover of Czechoslovakia and increased Soviet pressure on Berlin, six West European nations, meeting in Brussels, signed a fifty-year collective defensive treaty. Truman praised the treaty, saying that it deserved the "full support" of the United States.[26] On June 11, the Senate passed by a vote of sixty-four to six the Vandenberg Resolution, advising the president to seek security for America and the free world through U.S. support of mutual defense regional arrangements, including in Western Europe.

One week later, the Soviets responded by stopping all surface traffic of the Western allies in and out of Berlin. They then cut off all electricity, coal, food, and other supplies to West Berlin from East German territory under their control. The Berlin blockade had begun. After briefly considering and rejecting military action, the United States launched one of the most daring and successful operations of the Cold War—a massive airlift to supply the 2.25 million inhabitants of Berlin with the necessities of life.

Truman saw Berlin as the heart of the struggle over Germany and, in a larger sense, over Europe. He understood that "Berlin had become a symbol of America's—and the West's—dedication to the cause of freedom." He described the blockade as part of a Soviet plan to test the will and the capacity of the West to resist communist aggression. He did not want to start a war, but he refused to abandon the city.[27] He compared the Kremlin maneuver to its earlier probes in Greece and Turkey and considered both moves to have originated from the same communist ideology.

A reluctant Stalin finally ended the blockade eleven months later, on May 12, 1949, although the airlift continued until September 30 to build up stocks to deter further threats. Delivering 2.325 million tons of supplies in 277,804 flights, the United States had demonstrated to the Kremlin its resolve to stand by West Berlin and by extension West Germany and Western Europe. This was the policy of containment in action. In Carole K. Fink's words, in real as well as symbolic terms, the "'Berlin syndrome' wiped out the Munich nightmare that had haunted the West for a decade."[28]

In July 1948, shortly after the start of the Berlin crisis, Undersecretary of State Robert Lovett began discussions in Washington with the ambassadors of Great Britain, France, Belgium, the Netherlands, Luxembourg, and Canada on common security problems, discussions that would lead to the establishment of the North Atlantic Treaty Organization in April 1949.

Truman regarded NATO not merely as a military alliance but as one more step in the creation of an American foreign policy, along with the UN charter, the Truman Doctrine, and the Marshall Plan, calculated to contain Soviet imperialism and protect global freedom and justice through free peoples and open, representative governments. The North Atlantic Treaty's preamble declared that its signatories were "determined to safeguard the freedom, common heritage, and civilization of their peoples, founded on the principles of democracy, individual liberty, and the rule of law."[29]

Some critics, such as George Kennan, thought that U.S. foreign policy had gone as far as it should with the Truman Doctrine and the Marshall Plan, but the president did not agree. Political and economic aid, he believed, was insufficient to meet the unprecedented demands of the Cold War; a strategic military component was needed as part of containment. As the communists continued to apply pressure to Western Europe in the mid-to-late 1940s, Truman saw a world made dangerous by the Soviet Union. He hoped that the Atlantic alliance would defend its members against Soviet belligerence and possible invasion. He had greater hopes for NATO's overall contribution to containment.[30]

In a confidential discussion with NATO foreign ministers in April 1949, Truman made it clear that in his mind, the North Atlantic Treaty embodied the West's resolve to fight communist ideology with a strategic organization. Because NATO's "best estimate is that we have several years in which we can count on a breathing spell" before the Soviets acquired atomic weapons, the president assumed that the Atlantic alliance could safely rely for the time on conventional forces for its defense. This assumption would change abruptly with the Soviet explosion of an atom bomb in September 1949. But in any case, NATO by itself was insufficient. Truman regarded the political, economic, and military pieces of containment as interdependent and the overall strategy as anything but passive. He told the foreign ministers, "We should appreciate that Soviet nationalism is dynamic; it must expand, and the only way to defeat it eventually is not merely to contain it but to carry the ideological war to the Soviet sphere itself."[31]

The Soviet Union made no further conquests in Western Europe or the Near East after its post-war military occupation of Eastern and Central Europe. But containment was not employed early enough in the Far East for several reasons.

Neither President Truman nor Secretary of State Acheson knew as much about Asia as he did about Europe. Because Marshall had spent time in the Philippines and China—most recently for a year as the president's special ambassador to China—the president and his secretary of state deferred to the great wartime general. Following Marshall's lead, Truman thought that Chiang Kai-shek and the Nationalist Chinese were little better than Mao Zedong and the Chinese communists. He was unwilling to do more in terms of military supplies or economic aid to "save" China, given its size and the failure of previous U.S. aid. China fell in the fall of 1949 to the communists, triggering the Republican charge that the Democrats had "lost" China.

WHO LOST CHINA?

In February 1949, Acheson and Ambassador-at-Large Philip Jessup proposed to Truman that military supplies then being loaded in ships to Hawaii and San Francisco for Chiang Kai-shek's government be stopped as a move toward peace in China. Senator Vandenberg, present at the meeting, wrote in his diary: "If, at the very moment when Chiang's Nationalists are desperately trying to negotiate some kind of peace with the Communists, we suspend all military shipments to the Nationalists, we certainly shall make any hope of negotiated peace impossible. We shall thus virtually notify the Communists that they can consider the war ended and themselves as victors."[32]

John K. Fairbank, Harvard's renowned China scholar, and other supporters of a pro-Mao U.S. policy, argued that Chiang's defeat was inevitable and that Marshall "succeeded in preventing the Americans from going into a super-Vietnam to quell the Chinese Revolution."[33] But the suggestion that opponents of the Chinese communists and supporters of the Nationalist Chinese—like Congressman Walter Judd—sought the entry of thousands if not millions of American troops is far off the mark. What they urged was adequate U.S. military and economic aid to China, not American forces. They understood the impossibility of America's winning a land war in Asia, as President Lyndon Johnson later showed he did not in Vietnam.

Truman, however, did not embrace the new communist China. Responding to the suggestion from the State Department that the United States officially recognize the People's Republic of China, Truman said that as long he was president "that cut-throat organization will not be recognized by us."[34] Truman's flat rejection came after the launch of the Korean War, in which the PRC bore substantial responsibility for the loss of American life (an estimated thirty-eight thousand American servicemen died in Korea).

THE BAMBOO CURTAIN

In October 1949, when Mao Zedong proclaimed the birth of the People's Republic of China, a Bamboo Curtain descended on some 540 million Chinese just as an Iron Curtain had descended across the European continent. In the following decades, two great communist powers, the PRC and the Soviet Union, usually but not always cooperated in advancing Marxism-Leninism while competing for the leadership of the communist world.

In both countries, Marxist-Leninist ideology was an essential element that gave the Communist Party absolute power and ensured its control of domestic and foreign policy. Ideology bred many of the same totalitarian practices in both countries:

- Slave labor camps—the Gulag in the Soviet Union, the laogai in China.
- Forced famines—the Holodomor in Ukraine and other parts of the Soviet Union, the so-called Great Leap Forward in China.
- The political role of the military—the Red Army in the Soviet Union, the People's Liberation Army in China.
- The cult of personality—Stalin in the USSR, Mao in China.
- Mass terror—the Great Terror (1936–1938) in the Soviet Union, the Great Cultural Revolution in China (1966–1976).
- Indifference to the deaths of those who resisted or even questioned communism, resulting in an estimated twenty million victims in the Soviet Union and as many as sixty million victims in China.

The key to understanding both the Soviet Union and Communist China, asserts the historian Martin Malia, is ideology. It is only by taking the communists at their ideological word, "treating their socialist utopia with literal-minded seriousness, that we can grasp the tragedy to which it led."[35] In *The Gulag Archipelago*, Aleksandr Solzhenitsyn writes that "the imagination and inner strength of Shakespeare's villains stopped short at ten or so cadavers. Because they had no ideology." Not so the communists: "It is thanks to ideology that it fell to the lot of the twentieth century to experience villainy on a scale of millions."[36]

NSC 68

The prospect in 1950 of a united and expansionist communism, led by the Soviet Union and Communist China, led the Truman administration to draft and adopt the most important national security document of the Cold War—National Security Council Report 68.

In late January 1950, Truman requested an in-depth report on the continuing world crisis. Drafted by Paul Nitze, who had replaced George Kennan as the director of the State Department's Policy Planning Staff, and a team of State and Defense Department officials, NSC 68 was submitted to the president in April.

Truman was reacting to a series of aggressive communist actions, including the Soviet organization in

January 1949 of the Council of Mutual Economic Assistance (Comecon), intended to strengthen the USSR's hold on Eastern Europe; the successful Soviet test in September of an atom bomb; the establishment of the People's Republic of China; the creation of the communist German Democratic Republic (East Germany); and Mao's public promise that China would side with the Soviet Union in the event of a third world war.

Of special concern to the president was the Soviet explosion of an atomic bomb, which the administration had not expected until mid-1950 at the earliest. Truman quickly decided that the United States should proceed with the development of a hydrogen bomb. He defined the key components of American military strength as a modernized and trained conventional capacity and a nuclear edge over the communists.

NSC 68 presented Truman with a comprehensive plan of action to meet the Soviet challenge. The plan would serve as America's core strategy until superseded by President Richard Nixon's policy of détente in the early 1970s.

In its first section, NSC 68 describes the USSR as a tyranny with an unprecedented ambition: "The Soviet Union, unlike previous aspirants to hegemony, is animated by a new fanatic faith, antithetical to our own, and seeks to impose its absolute authority over the rest of the world." It sketches the violent and nonviolent means at Moscow's disposal as well as the possible use of atomic weapons. The document agrees with Truman's view that the Soviets acted ideologically and with irrational suspicion at the same time.[37]

In the second and third sections, NSC 68 compares America's fundamental purpose and the Soviet Union's ideological objective. Citing the Declaration of Independence, the Constitution, and the Bill of Rights, it argues that America has striven "to assure the integrity and vitality of our free society, which is founded upon the dignity and worth of the individual." Without apology, America considers itself to be a good regime.

In sharp contrast, the Kremlin is driven by the desire to achieve absolute power and extend it over the non-Soviet world. Communist ideology requires the enslavement not the fostering of the individual. The Soviets' primary strategic target is the United States, the bulwark of opposition to Soviet expansion.

The fourth section of NSC 68 contrasts the idea of freedom under a government of laws with the idea of slavery under a despotic government. The document argues that the Soviet blend of domestic insularity and overall aggression is primarily the product of Marxism-Leninism, not historic Russian insecurity.

NSC 68 stresses the global nature of the Cold War, making the frequently quoted observation, "The assault on free institutions is world-wide now...and a defeat of free institutions anywhere is a defeat everywhere." The document outlines a wide-ranging strategy to meet communist imperialism. The primary goal is to maintain a strong free world—politically, morally, economically, and militarily—and to frustrate the Soviet design and bring about its internal change.

In the fifth section, NSC 68 examines Soviet intentions and capabilities. The Soviet Union is inescapably a military threat because "it possesses and is possessed by a world-wide revolutionary movement, because it is the inheritor of Russian imperialism, and because it is a totalitarian dictatorship." Communist doctrine "dictates the employment of violence, subversion and deceit, and rejects moral considerations."[38]

The Truman administration saw Soviet intentions and capabilities as interlaced. Had Truman gauged capabilities with no reference to ideology and intentions, he might have given way to the Soviets in Berlin rather than ordering the airlift.

The primary Soviet weakness identified by NSC 68 is the nature of its relationship with the peoples of the USSR. The Iron Curtain surrounding the satellite nations holds together the Soviet empire. The document looks to the independence of nationalities as a natural and potent threat to communism.

In the sixth section, NSC 68 contrasts U.S. intentions and capabilities with those of the Soviet Union. A thriving global community, including economic prosperity, is necessary for the American system to flourish. For the Soviets to join the system, they would have to abandon their imperialist designs.

Containment is defined as blocking further expansion of Soviet power, exposing communist ideology, weakening the Kremlin's control and influence, and fostering the seeds of destruction within the Soviet system. At the same time, NSC 68 leaves open the possibility of U.S. negotiations with the Soviet Union—but from a position of American strength.

The last section of NSC 68 endorses Truman's commitment to peace within a program of increased political, economic, and military power (including atomic weapons). The buildup constitutes a firm policy "to check and to roll back the Kremlin drive for world domination."

Recognizing the possible dangers of such a policy, the report insists that a free people must be willing and able to defend its freedom.

Just as the Truman Doctrine, the Marshall Plan, and NATO had done, NSC 68 calls for a free world to which, at a minimum, the Soviet Union must adjust. Rather than coexisting with the USSR, it argues, the free world's combined strength—made up of democracies under the rule of law, with open markets, and rooted in Western principles—would transform the Soviet system. NSC 68 was the definitive statement of the U.S. strategy to expose and act against communist tyranny whenever and wherever possible—a strategy that would soon be seriously tested.[39]

THREE

THE HOT WARS OF THE COLD WAR
(1950–1973)

During the 1950s and the 1960s, Presidents Dwight D. Eisenhower and John F. Kennedy essentially followed Truman's policy of containment, seeing the Cold War as a protracted conflict between the United States, representing the free world, and the Soviet Union, representing the non-free world. Whenever the Soviets or their surrogates attempted to extend the communist sphere of influence, U.S. leaders, whether Republican or Democratic, responded, resorting to military action when it was deemed necessary.

THE KOREAN WAR (1950–1953)

Toward the end of World War II, Korea, which had been forcibly annexed by Japan in the early twentieth century, was divided across the middle, along the thirty-eighth parallel, the northern part occupied by the Soviet Union, the southern part by the United States. Following Japan's surrender, Soviet troops evacuated North Korea, leaving behind them the "Democratic People's Republic of Korea," headed by Kim Il Sung, a Moscow-trained communist. American troops then withdrew from the South, led by the firmly anti-communist Syngman Rhee.

In January 1950, while discussing vital U.S. security interests in the Pacific area, Secretary of State Acheson spoke of a "defensive perimeter" that ran along the Aleutians to Japan and the Ryukyu Islands and then to the Philippines. He described these islands as "essential parts" of the Pacific area that "must and will be held." Because he did not specifically mention Korea, many observers (including the communists) assumed that the United States would not come to its aid if attacked. They should have read what Acheson said at the conclusion of his remarks "about the military security of other areas in the Pacific": "Should such an attack occur...the initial reliance must be on the people attacked to resist it and then upon the commitments of the entire civilized world under the Charter of the United Nations."[1] Eager to take advantage of what he wrongly perceived to be American indifference to Korea's security, Kim Il Sung pressed Stalin hard for permission to "liberate" South Korea. In February, Stalin ordered the preparation of a "Preemptive Strike Operations Plan" and on June 10 gave Kim the final go-ahead. The Soviets prepared a cover story: the United States was allegedly developing an attack plan against North Korea to be executed in the summer of 1950 by some one hundred thousand South Korean troops armed by the United States.[2] There was in fact no such U.S. plan.

On June 25, 1950, a large North Korean army invaded the South and soon controlled most of the lower part of the Korean peninsula. As we now know from documents in the Kremlin archives, Stalin not only approved the invasion but provided substantial military and economic assistance to Kim, including up-to-date Soviet motorized equipment, artillery, aircraft, and manpower.[3]

The communists expected no American interference in their imperial plans. But when informed of the invasion, Truman said to Acheson, "Dean, we've got to stop the sons-of-bitches no matter what."[4] He ordered an emergency session of his military and foreign policy advisors, who decided South Korea had to be defended both for the sake of its people and because of its strategic position across the straits from Japan. In accordance with NSC 68's philosophy that a defeat of free institutions anywhere is a defeat everywhere, the president ordered General Douglas MacArthur, based in Japan, to counter the communist tide; he also asked for action by the United Nations Security Council.[5] The council ordered North Korea to desist and called on all UN members to come to the aid of South Korea. Ten members, led by the United States, eventually did. Since January 1950, the Soviet representative had been boycotting meetings of the Security Council because China's seat was still occupied by the Republic of China (Taiwan). The Soviet Union could not therefore veto Truman's moves to commit the UN to the defense of South Korea.

Truman placed the fighting in Korea in the broader context of "the struggle between freedom and Communist slavery." While not playing down the military aspect of the Cold War, the president talked at a White House conference on children and youth about the moral and spiritual dangers of communist ideology: "Communism attacks our main basic values, our belief in God, our belief in the dignity of man and the value of human life, our belief in justice and freedom. It attacks the institutions that are based on these values. It attacks our churches, our guarantees of civil liberty, our courts, our democratic form of government." The president wanted the American people to understand, as fully and deeply as they could, the larger meaning of the Cold War.[6]

Under MacArthur's leadership, UN forces began a counteroffensive that by mid-November had brought its forces deep into North Korea and close to the Yalu River and the Chinese border. To MacArthur's surprise, the People's Republic of China launched a massive counterattack, sending two hundred thousand Chinese troops across the Yalu River against the outnumbered American forces.

Forced to retreat, the American army was soon once again below the thirty-eighth parallel. By mid-March 1951, however, with heavy reinforcements and naval command of both coasts and under a new field commander, General James Van Fleet, the U.S.-UN army recaptured Seoul and recovered South Korea to just above the thirty-eighth parallel, a return to the status quo before the North Korean invasion.

For Douglas MacArthur, however, there was no substitute for victory. Ignoring a presidential order to make no public statements, MacArthur personally wrecked a U.S. armistice initiative by threatening that if the Chinese did not withdraw at once, they would be "forced to their knees."[7] With the concurrence of the Joint Chiefs of Staff and his secretary of state, Truman on April 11, 1951, dismissed General MacArthur, a great American general with an even greater ego.

Armistice negotiations between North Korea and the United Nations began on July 10, 1951, and continued until March 1953, when the North Koreans finally agreed to an armed truce. No formal peace treaty has ever been signed. Regarding the repatriation of North Korean prisoners, the UN command rejected the communists' demand that all of them be returned to North Korea. Every prisoner was allowed to decide his destination. Three out of four elected to stay in the South, a damning indictment of the communist regime. Some historians have described the outcome of the Korea war as a "tie," but the eventual remarkable economic success and vibrant democracy of South Korea suggest strongly that it was a war worth fighting.

EISENHOWER AND CONTAINMENT

Dwight D. Eisenhower, revered as a heroic wartime leader, served as army chief of staff, president of Columbia University, and the first supreme commander of NATO. After growing up in a large, hardworking, religious family in Kansas, he attended West Point, and his subsequent military career made him a general's general. When he turned to politics, he eventually became a Republican, although both parties and all Americans wanted to claim him. As president of the United States, he combined a steely resolve against communist aggression, exploitation, and manipulation with a deep desire for global peace that flowed in part from his Christian faith (raised in the Brethren in Christ Church and baptized Presbyterian in 1953).

Shortly after Stalin's death in March 1953, Eisenhower gave a speech notably titled "The Chance for Peace," in which he made clear that the United States and its friends had chosen one road while Soviet leaders had chosen another path in the postwar world.[8] But he always looked for ways to encourage the Kremlin to move in a new direction. In a diary entry from January 1956, he summarized his national security policy, which became known as the "New Look": "We have tried to keep constantly before us the purpose of promoting peace with accompanying step-by-step disarmament. As a preliminary, of course, we have to induce the Soviets to agree to some form of inspection, in order that both sides may be confident that treaties are being executed faithfully. In the meantime, and pending some advance in this direction, we must stay strong, particularly in that type of power that the Russians are compelled to respect."[9]

One of Eisenhower's first acts upon taking office in January 1953 was to order a review of U.S. foreign policy. He generally agreed with Truman's approach to containment except for China, which he included in his strategic considerations. Task forces studied and made recommendations regarding three possible strategies:

1. A continuation of containment, the basic policy during the Truman years;

2. A policy of global deterrence, in which U.S. commitments would be expanded and communist aggression forcibly met;

3. A policy of liberation which through political, economic, and paramilitary means would "roll back" the communist empire and liberate the peoples behind the Iron and Bamboo Curtains.

The latter two options were favored by Secretary of State John Foster Dulles, who counseled the use of the *threat* of nuclear weapons to counter Soviet military force. He argued that having resolved the problem of military defense, the free world "could undertake what has been too long delayed—a political offensive."[10]

Eisenhower rejected liberation as too aggressive and containment as he understood it as too passive, selecting instead deterrence, with an emphasis on air and sea power. But he allowed Dulles to convey an impression of "deterrence plus." In January 1954, for example, Dulles proposed a new American policy—"a maximum deterrent at a bearable cost," in which "local defenses must be reinforced by the further deterrent of massive retaliatory power." The best way to deter aggression, Dulles said, is for "the free community to be willing and able to respond vigorously at places and with means of its own choosing."[11]

As the defense analysts James Jay Carafano and Paul Rosenzweig have observed, Eisenhower built his Cold War foreign policy on four pillars:

- Providing security through "a strong mix of both offensive and defensive means."
- Maintaining a robust economy.
- Preserving a civil society that would "give the nation the will to persevere during the difficult days of a long war."

- Winning the struggle of ideas against "a corrupt vacuous ideology" destined to fail its people.[12]

The Eisenhower-Dulles New Look was not, as some have charged, a policy with only two options—the use of local forces or nuclear threats. Covert means were used to help overthrow the pro-Marxist regime of Jacobo Arbenz Guzman in Guatemala in 1954, economic pressures were exerted in the Suez Crisis of 1956, and U.S. Marines were used in Lebanon in 1958. The U.S. Navy was deployed in the Taiwan Straits as part of Eisenhower's ongoing, staunch commitment to the protection of the Nationalist Chinese islands of Quemoy and Matsu—and by extension the Republic of China itself, Japan, and the Philippines—against communist aggression.[13] With the president's full endorsement, Dulles put alliance ahead of nuclear weapons as the "cornerstone of security for the free nations."[14]

During the Eisenhower years, the United States constructed a powerful ring of alliances and treaties around the communist empire. They included a strengthened NATO in Europe; the Eisenhower Doctrine (announced in 1957, protecting Middle Eastern countries from direct and indirect communist aggression); the Baghdad Pact, joining Turkey, Iraq, Great Britain, Pakistan, and Iran in the Middle East; the Southeast Asia Treaty Organization, which included the Philippines, Thailand, Australia, and New Zealand; mutual security agreements with South Korea and with the Republic of China; and a revised Rio Pact, with a pledge to resist communist subversion in Latin America.[15] As Eisenhower said in his first inaugural address, echoing NSC 68, "Freedom is pitted against slavery; lightness against the dark." Like Truman, he believed that freedom—rooted in eternal truths, natural law, equality, and inalienable rights—was the foundation for real peace, and he sharpened the idea that faith in this freedom ultimately united everyone: "Conceiving the defense of freedom, like freedom itself, to be one and indivisible, we hold all continents and peoples in equal regard and honor."[16]

Dulles, who had closely studied Soviet history and shared Eisenhower's deep Christian faith, regarded the very existence of the communist world as a threat to the United States. While George Kennan argued that communist ideology was an instrument not a determinant of Soviet policy, Dulles argued the opposite. The Soviet objective, Dulles said flatly, was global state socialism.

Eisenhower agreed: "Anyone who doesn't recognize that the great struggle of our time is an ideological one... [is] not looking the question squarely in the face."[17]

The common thread running through all the elements of the Eisenhower strategy—nuclear deterrence, alliances, psychological warfare, covert action, and negotiations—was a relatively low cost and an emphasis on retaining the initiative. The New Look was "an integrated and reasonably efficient adoption of resources to objectives, of means to ends."[18]

Not all of Eisenhower's challenges were external—some originated within the borders of the United States and indeed his own Republican party. The most visible and contentious problem was how to deal with the outspoken, unpredictable Senator Joseph McCarthy of Wisconsin.

SENATOR JOSEPH McCARTHY

McCarthy was a conservative backbencher when he journeyed to Wheeling, West Virginia, in February 1950 to make a speech in which he declared, without providing any hard evidence or names, that a number of communists were currently employed by the State Department. From that day until December 1954, when the Senate voted to censure his conduct, McCarthy was at the center of the American political stage.

To millions of Americans, he was the uncompromising champion of anticommunism. To many others, he came to be seen as a reckless character assassin. A new word—"McCarthyism," the making of baseless accusations—was coined by his enemies. Defiant supporters wore the label proudly.

McCarthy made his charges in a tense political atmosphere. The United States had seen the fall of China to the communists, the trials and conviction of the one-time Soviet spy Alger Hiss, the spy cases of Julius and Ethel Rosenberg and Klaus Fuchs, and the communist invasion of South Korea. As Irving Kristol, the godfather of neoconservatism, wrote in 1952 in the then-liberal journal *Commentary*, "There is one thing the American people know about Senator McCarthy: he, like them, is unequivocally anti-Communist. About the spokesmen for American liberalism, they feel they know no such thing."[19]

But McCarthy had a fatal flaw: he rarely listened to anyone, even his closest friends and advisers, particularly when they counseled patience and prudence. Whittaker Chambers expressed his deep concern about McCarthy to William F. Buckley Jr., calling the senator "a slugger and a rabble-rouser" who "simply knows that someone threw a tomato and the general direction from which it came." McCarthy, he said, had only one tactic—"attack"—and that was not sufficient.[20]

The senator's decline began in the late summer and early fall of 1953 when he took on the Eisenhower administration and the Pentagon. McCarthy, now the chairman of the Senate Permanent Subcommittee on Investigations, objected to the promotion of a commissioned army officer named Irving Peress, who had invoked the Fifth Amendment when given a loyalty form asking about possible communist party membership. (He was subsequently identified as a communist organizer.)

Brigadier General Ralph W. Zwicker, Peress's commanding officer, was summoned by McCarthy to appear before his subcommittee and explain the army's action. Infuriated by the general's evasive answers, McCarthy declared that Zwicker, a highly decorated veteran of World War II, was "not fit" to wear the uniform. An angry President Eisenhower, who had commended Zwicker for his wartime service, decided it was time to take action against McCarthy.

With White House approval, a Senate investigation of McCarthy's subcommittee was ordered. The result was the celebrated Army-McCarthy hearings, which were televised live in the spring of 1954 to an estimated daily audience of twenty million people.

McCarthy was correct about some things. In the 1930s and 1940s, there was a high-level network of communist spies, such as Harry Dexter White and Alger Hiss, in the American government. Eighty-one State Department employees identified by McCarthy as security risks left the government through dismissal or resignation. Unlikely observers agreed there had been communists in the government. In his memoirs, George Kennan writes:

> The penetration of the American governmental services by members or agents (conscious or otherwise) of the American Communist Party in the late 1930s was not a figment of the imagination of the hysterical right-wingers of a later decade. Stimulated and facilitated by the events of the Depression, particularly on the younger intelligentsia, it really existed, and it assumed proportions which, while never overwhelming,

were also not trivial.… [B]y the end of the war, so far as I can judge from the evidence I have seen, the penetration was quite extensive.[21]

Nevertheless, the Senate voted sixty-seven to twenty-two to censure McCarthy for his conduct. He disappeared from the front pages and died three years later, at the age of forty-eight, apparently from alcoholism.

McCarthy's investigations, nevertheless, forced changes in military policy that tightened up security and made communist infiltration of the army more difficult. President Eisenhower himself admitted that the army had made "serious errors" in its handling of the Peress case.[22]

The McCarthy subcommittee on investigations was the first investigative agency to expose the murder, torture, starvation, and inhuman treatment of captured American personnel by North Korean and Chinese communist troops during the Korean War. Twenty-nine witnesses, including twenty-three survivors or eyewitnesses of communist atrocities, added their evidence to affidavits, statements, photographs, and official war records. About two-thirds of the American servicemen taken prisoner died from acts of barbarism.

The subsequent release of secret Kremlin documents in the early 1990s confirmed that the American Communist Party had been controlled and financed by the Soviet Communist Party prior to and during the Cold War. According to the historians Harvey Klehr, John Earl Haynes, and Fridrikh Igorevich Firsov, the documents demonstrate that the "widespread popular belief that many American Communists collaborated with Soviet intelligence and placed loyalty to the Soviet Union ahead of loyalty to the United States was well founded." And furthermore, the "concern about the subversive threat of the [Communist Party of the United States of America] and worries that Communists employed in sensitive government jobs constituted a security risk were equally well founded."[23]

HUNGARY AND SUEZ

Eisenhower was president at a time, said Congressman Walter Judd, when the world was "filled with confusion," when a third of its people had gained their independence, and a third had lost it. "No such convulsions have ever previously occurred in all of human history."[24] Yet for the majority of Americans, the Eisenhower years went by so calmly—at least until the Soviets shot down an American U-2 spy plane in 1960—that they did not realize what serious dangers had been overcome. Still, there was some criticism of Eisenhower's foreign policy, particularly the U.S. response to the Hungarian uprising of 1956.

On October 22, 1956, five thousand students crammed into a hall in Budapest and approved a manifesto that, among other things, called for the withdrawal of Soviet troops from Hungary, free elections, freedom of association, and economic reform. The following day, thousands filled the streets of the capital city, chanting "Russians go home!" and ending up in Hero Square, where they pulled down a giant statue of Stalin.[25]

"In twelve brief days of euphoria and chaos," writes the historian Anne Applebaum, "nearly every symbol of the communist regime was attacked" and, in most cases, destroyed. Along with eight thousand other political prisoners, Cardinal Joseph Mindszenty was released from the prison in which he had been kept in solitary confinement. Hungarian soldiers deserted in droves and gave their weapons to the revolutionaries. But then Soviet tanks and troops rolled back into the city in the first days of November, brutally crushing the revolution and killing an estimated two thousand people. Nearly fifteen thousand were wounded. According to the authoritative *Black Book of Communism*, thirty-five thousand people were arrested, twenty-two thousand jailed, and two hundred executed. More than two hundred thousand Hungarians fled the country, many of them to America.[26]

Conservatives charged that the Eisenhower administration, after encouraging resistance if not revolution, failed to help the Hungarian freedom fighters. In some of its broadcasts, Radio Free Europe, financed by the U.S. government and run by Eastern European exiles, gave the impression that the West might come to the Hungarians' assistance. It didn't. There were several reasons why America did not act in Hungary:

- The United States asked Austria for freedom of passage to get to Hungary, but Vienna refused transit by land or even use of its air space.
- The United States had no plan for dealing with any major uprising behind the Iron Curtain. No one in authority apparently believed that something like the Hungarian Revolution might happen.

- The Soviets had the home-field advantage,
  and an American defeat would have been a
  serious strategic defeat not only in Europe
  but around the world.

Outwardly unsuccessful, the Hungarian Revolution showed that communism in Eastern Europe was weaker than anyone, including the communists, realized. An empire viewed by many in the West as invincible was exposed as vulnerable.

On October 29, 1956—in the middle of the Hungarian Revolution—Israel attacked Egypt, sparking the Suez Crisis and exposing major divisions in the West. Britain and France vetoed a UN Security Council cease-fire resolution offered by the United States and the Soviet Union and then joined the Israeli effort to depose Egypt's anti-Western leader, Gamal Nasser, and secure Western control of the Suez Canal.

The fighting continued for another five days, during which the Soviets crushed the Hungarian revolt, having calculated that the West, particularly the United States, would be too preoccupied with Suez to take any action in Hungary. With Dulles in the hospital, Eisenhower took personal charge of U.S. foreign policy and applied economic and political pressure on Britain to force a cease-fire in the Middle East. The communists were thus denied the opportunity to link the United States with the "colonialist" position of Great Britain and France.

KHRUSHCHEV AND DE-STALINIZATION

The Eisenhower administration was also required to factor into its foreign policy calculations Nikita Khrushchev's dramatic "de-Stalinization" speech in February 1956. After a succession crisis following Stalin's death in 1953, Khrushchev, as general secretary of the Communist Party, decided to open a box long closed even to party members. Although the speech before the Twentieth Party Congress was supposed to be secret, leaks soon occurred through the comments of foreign communist leaders who had been present. Its startling contents made headlines in the West.

In language that was blunt even for him, Khrushchev disclosed that torture had been extensively used to extract so-called confessions from former colleagues of Stalin, thousands of innocent persons had been executed at Stalin's orders, and Stalin had been responsible for the ruthless mass deportation of ethnic minorities during World War II.

Khrushchev attacked Stalin's "megalomania" and "self-glorification," which led to the "cult of personality." He derided Stalin's military ability and wartime leadership—heretofore praised to the skies—and pointed out that the great leader had ignored repeated warnings in 1941 that the Germans were about to attack the Soviet Union.

Notwithstanding its anti-Stalin theme, Khrushchev's speech was not a repudiation of Soviet communism but a criticism of Stalin's misuse of it. Khrushchev never publicly apologized for the mass murders he privately condemned before the Soviet Congress. In fact, as first secretary of the Moscow party organization, he had been part of the Great Terror of 1937–1938. As Ukraine's first secretary, he had implemented Stalin's forced famine in Ukraine and elsewhere in the Soviet Union in the early 1930s. He never repudiated Stalinism, telling the Chinese in 1957 that to be a communist was "inseparable from being a Stalinist."[27]

Paradoxically, in the same year that he condemned Stalin for being Stalin, Khrushchev employed Stalinist tactics against dissidents in Poland and Hungary, ruthlessly crushing their attempts to obtain freedom. Some Soviets saw Khrushchev's speech as a call for reform, but when they spoke out in favor of democratization and against Stalinist excesses, thousands were arrested and deported to the Gulag. The leading Western historian of Stalinist Russia, Robert Conquest, estimated that while several million prisoners in the labor camps were "rehabilitated" under Khrushchev, four million remained in the Gulag.

As to ideology, Khrushchev told fellow communists that "peaceful coexistence" meant continuation of the Marxist-Leninist strategy of communizing the world by other means. He endorsed wars of national liberation in Africa and elsewhere. He even conducted his own purges, although they were less immediately terminal than Stalin's—army officers not sufficiently loyal to him were summarily fired and given no hope of obtaining a civilian job or a pension.[28]

As Martin Malia has written, the fundamental structures of a totalitarian state remained in place—the party-state, central economic planning, the political police (KGB), and a system of party cells at every level of society—all subordinated to the goal "of building and defending 'real socialism.'"[29]

One unquestioned Soviet triumph of the period was the launching of the Sputnik satellite in October 1957.

The American public and many U.S. officials were badly shaken by its successful flight. Despite heated talk about a "missile gap," Eisenhower refused to increase the number of U.S. long-range missiles, since reconnaissance flights over Russia showed that the United States enjoyed a sizeable advantage in intercontinental ballistic missiles.

THE CUBAN CHALLENGE

The Eisenhower administration was more concerned about a problem only ninety miles from America's shores. With the ascension in January 1959 of Fidel Castro in Cuba, the future of freedom in the Western hemisphere came into question. Official Washington was not yet certain about the political philosophy of the new Cuban leader, but the wholesale executions of those who had opposed Castro followed the communist pattern in other countries. In the spring of 1960, Eisenhower instructed the Pentagon and the CIA to draw up plans for the liberation of Cuba. The president was not committed to any particular course but aimed to honor the Monroe Doctrine and protect the Western hemisphere from any dangerous foreign influence.

In August 1960, a close Castro adviser brought a letter to Moscow: the Cuban dictator wanted to announce the creation of a Marxist party and to seek solidarity with the Soviets. That fall, Castro and Khrushchev both attended the general assembly of the United Nations in New York, where the Soviet leader publicly embraced his Cuban comrade.

By November 1960, a U.S. invasion plan was almost complete, and Eisenhower expected that it would be carried out by a victorious President Richard Nixon. When John F. Kennedy was elected instead, Eisenhower told the president-elect about the ominous Cuban situation and said, "We got into this mess under my administration. I'm prepared to go ahead and take action right now in these remaining two months of my term and clean this thing up down there in Cuba." Kennedy rejected the offer, saying, "No, the people have spoken. They have chosen me as president. Any decision on this must be left for me in my administration. We'll hope to find some other way." Eisenhower later told a confidant that one of the worst mistakes he made as president was not implementing the plan for invading Cuba and toppling Castro.[30]

U.S.-Soviet relations were further complicated in 1960 by the U-2 incident. A one-man aircraft with a single turbo jet engine capable of flying at an altitude of sixty-five thousand feet, the U-2 had been taking incredibly detailed photographs of the Soviet Union for the CIA since 1956. CIA analysts could read a newspaper headline nine miles below the aircraft. It was thought that the U-2 flew above the range of Soviet radar and missiles.

On May 1, 1960, two weeks before Eisenhower and Khrushchev were to hold a summit meeting in Paris with the leaders of Great Britain and France, a U-2 piloted by Francis Gary Powers was shot down by a Soviet rocket deep within the Soviet Union. When Khrushchev charged the United States with "aggressive acts," the State Department responded mendaciously that there was no "deliberate intention" to violate Soviet air space.

Khrushchev then released photos of the downed plane and revealed that Powers had made a complete confession. Secretary of State Christian Herter was forced to concede that the president had approved the program but not specific flights, which he said would continue. Khrushchev escalated the rhetoric, warning that Soviet rockets would attack countries that allowed U.S. spy planes to use their territory and said that Powers would be tried for spying.

Still hoping to go to Moscow for a summit meeting with Khrushchev, Eisenhower announced that the U-2 flights had been suspended and would not be resumed during his presidency, but he refused to apologize. An angry Khrushchev accused the president of "treachery" and "bandit acts" and canceled his invitation to the president to visit the Soviet Union. A grim Eisenhower reiterated that the U-2 would fly no more (U-2 flights resumed under President Kennedy) but declared that the Soviet premier's ultimatum regarding apologies and punishment of those responsible for the flights was unacceptable. Taking up an issue that would have been discussed at a summit, Khrushchev announced that the Soviet Union would solve the Berlin problem by signing a separate peace treaty with East Germany.[31]

If we compare the Cold War policies of Truman and Eisenhower, we see that both followed a policy of generally strong responses to the Soviet Union. Taken together, they left a legacy of resolve that the communists would not take more territory and peoples than they already had. With U.S. superiority in nuclear weapons, a strong NATO, and the development of highly sophisticated satellite reconnaissance during the Eisenhower years, the United States was seemingly in a position to win a protracted struggle. Notwithstanding the anticommunist outbursts in East Germany in 1953 and Poland in 1956 and the Hungarian uprising in 1956, the United States softened its diplomatic relations with a post-Stalin Soviet Union. Despite continuity with Truman's containment in several key areas, the Eisenhower administration laid the groundwork for a possible shift in U.S. strategy with more emphasis on summitry, negotiations, and compromise with the Kremlin.

KENNEDY VS. KHRUSHCHEV

In his eloquent inaugural address in 1961, a young and charismatic President John F. Kennedy declared that "the torch has been passed to a new generation of Americans—born in this century, tempered by war, disciplined by a hard and bitter peace." He spoke of a trumpet that summoned America "to bear the burden of a long twilight struggle" against "tyranny, poverty, disease, and war itself." He made this unequivocal vow, echoing Truman and Eisenhower:

> Let every nation know, whether it wishes us well or ill, that we shall pay any price, bear any burden, meet any hardship, support any friend, oppose any foe to assure the survival and success of liberty.[32]

As a candidate for president, Kennedy had signaled his strong belief that America faced an international crisis. In September 1960 he said that "to be an American in the next decade will be a hazardous experience. We will live on the edge of danger." In the following weeks, he intensified his rhetoric, saying, "Freedom and communism are locked in deadly embrace." The issue, he said, was the "preservation of civilization…. The world cannot exist half slave and half free."[33] Although a generation younger than Truman and Eisenhower, Kennedy, a Roman Catholic, shared their anticommunism and was known for his pro–defense spending record as a Democratic congressman and then senator from Massachusetts. Some of his judgment about the Cold War stemmed from his World War II service in the navy, which earned him a Purple Heart for his heroism as the commander of PT 109 in the Pacific.

At the same time, Kennedy determined for political as well as strategic reasons to distance himself from his predecessor. There would be no single dominant foreign policy voice like Dulles—Kennedy deliberately cultivated a wide range of national security advisers.

The main difference between Kennedy and Eisenhower was a so-called transition from a strategic deterrent by missiles and bombers to a balanced buildup of navy, Marine Corps, and ground forces to deal with limited wars. But as we have seen, Eisenhower employed conventional and covert measures when necessary to assure national security. And Kennedy, as we will see, engaged in a nuclear test of wills with the Soviet Union. The consistency is not surprising and reaches back to Truman, for several key architects of NSC 68—including Paul Nitze and Dean Rusk—were influential in the decisions of the Kennedy administration.

The Soviet testing of the new president began almost immediately. After congratulating Kennedy for his assurance of peaceful intentions, Khrushchev renewed open-air nuclear testing. The president delayed his response but at last announced he had ordered the United States to resume testing.

Kennedy took seriously Khrushchev's pledge to support "wars of national liberation." He warned, "We are opposed around the world by a monolithic and ruthless conspiracy that relies primarily on covert means for expanding its sphere of influence." Throughout the 1960s, the terrain of the Cold War became truly global, ranging from Europe to Asia, Africa, and Latin America, with the possibility of nuclear war and the reality of guerrilla war, insurrection, and subversion.[34] Battles hot and cold were fought in Cuba, Berlin, and Vietnam.

One of the first engagements in this new stage of the Cold War took place in Cuba. In April 1961, a small force of about fifteen hundred anti-Castro Cubans (trained and armed by the CIA) landed at the Bay of Pigs in Cuba, hoping to spark a popular uprising against the communist government. On the eve of the operation, however, a vacillating Kennedy, concerned about too visible a U.S. role, cut by 80 percent the air support that was crucial to success. Available U.S. warships and aircraft were held back. The invasion was an abject failure, resulting in massive casualties and the capture of more than a thousand members of the invasion force. Analysts agree that Kennedy should have either provided adequate air and sea support or called off the operation.

At a June meeting in Vienna, Kennedy and Khrushchev took the measure of each other. The president concluded that America faced a ruthless opponent committed to advancing world communism through wars of national liberation. The seasoned Soviet leader was not impressed by the youthful American president and decided to challenge him.

On August 13, 1961, Khrushchev ordered the construction of a twenty-eight-mile-long concrete and brick wall dividing the city of Berlin into east and west. The draconian move was taken to stop the flood of tens of thousands of East Germans seeking freedom in the Western zone of Berlin. It took two years to complete the wall, which was topped with barbed wire and protected by minefields, police dogs, and guards with orders to shoot to kill anyone who tried to cross it. In the first year, sixty-four freedom seekers were killed by border guards—only a few escaped.

Strong protest notes about the wall were delivered to Moscow by the U.S., British, and French governments, but no military action followed aside from the arrival of fifteen hundred American troops and twenty motor vehicles as "reinforcements" for the U.S. garrison in West Berlin. Years later, Secretary of State Dean Rusk argued that any Allied attempt to interfere with the construction of the wall would have brought war. When he visited Berlin in 1963, President Kennedy pointedly said, "Freedom has many difficulties and democracy is not perfect, but we have never had to put a wall up to keep our people in, to prevent them from leaving us." He described the wall as "the most obvious and vivid demonstration of the failures of the Communist system, for all the world to see."[35] But in fact the unopposed building of the Berlin Wall was a significant Soviet victory. Before the wall, writes the foreign affairs analyst Brian Crozier, the drain of the population, including some of its most talented citizens, had threatened the survival of the East German state—"in economic terms the most important of the Soviet Union's imperial acquisitions."[36] The Berlin Wall would stand for another twenty-eight years.

An emboldened Khrushchev again tested Kennedy's mettle by attempting in the summer and fall of 1962 to deploy offensive nuclear missiles in Cuba and redress the nuclear imbalance between the USSR and the United States, which had a seventeen-to-one advantage in nuclear warheads. Also, Khrushchev and his colleagues were delighted that a communist revolution had occurred in Cuba without assistance from Moscow, seeming to confirm Marx's prediction about the course of history; they wanted to encourage other "revolutions" in Latin America. Soviet ships began unloading technicians, planes, and ballistic missiles. Cuban exiles informed members of Congress and administration officials that missile sites were being built. Soviet officials assured the Kennedy administration that the missiles were defensive. A concerned president ordered U-2 flights to determine what was really going on. Photos revealed short-range missiles that could hit targets from Washington to Panama and medium-range missiles with a range from Hudson Bay to Lima, Peru. Soviet ships with additional missiles on board were photographed headed to Cuba.

The president established an executive committee of the National Security Council to evaluate the escalating crisis and recommend an appropriate U.S. response. For Secretary of State Rusk and Secretary of Defense Robert McNamara, writes the historian Katherine A. S. Sibley, "the Munich analogy was compelling—the United States must not allow Soviet aggression as Europeans had appeased Hitler in 1938." A majority of the executive committee's members favored direct military action although not a full-scale invasion. Attorney General Robert Kennedy blocked the idea, arguing that if the United States followed such an offensive course, its moral position in the world would be destroyed. More practically, it was almost certain that Soviet troops would be killed, provoking a military response from Moscow. A consensus formed for a "quarantine" of Cuba, using over 180 American ships.[37]

On October 22, a stern-faced President Kennedy announced over national television that the United States was placing a quarantine around Cuba and demanded that the Soviets remove their nuclear missiles. For almost two weeks, the world wondered whether a nuclear war threatened. High priority messages flashed back and forth between Moscow and Washington. As tension mounted and U.S. forces, including sixty nuclear-loaded B-52s, were placed on high alert, the Soviets began dismantling the sites and shipping their missiles back to Russia. A chastened Khrushchev acknowledged the superior military strength, including nuclear weapons, of the United States.

But in return the United States publicly pledged that it would not invade Cuba, abandoning the Monroe Doctrine and giving Castro a safe base from which to disseminate communist agitation and propaganda in Latin America. Privately, the White House promised to remove U.S. intermediate-range missiles in Turkey, aimed at the Soviet Union, and nearly all of the forty-two thousand Soviet troops and experts in Cuba were allowed to remain. They began training a large Cuban army that engaged in anti-American operations in Africa and Asia in the late 1960s and throughout the 1970s.

VIETNAM

Halfway around the world, another Cold War conflict was escalating. The struggle for control of Vietnam, which had been a French colony since 1887, lasted for three decades. The first part of the war was between the French and the Vietminh, the Vietnamese nationalists led by the communist Ho Chi Minh, and continued from 1946 until 1954. The second part was between the United States and South Vietnam on one hand and North Vietnam and the National Liberation Front on the other, ending with the victory of the latter in 1975. The communist side, strongly backed by the Soviet Union and mainland China, sought to increase the number of those who lived behind the Bamboo Curtain.

Both the United States and the Soviet Union regarded the conflict not as a civil war between North and South Vietnam but as a consequential engagement of the Cold War in a strategic region. American leaders endorsed the domino theory, first enunciated by President Eisenhower, that if South Vietnam fell to the communists, other nations in the region such as Laos and Cambodia would also fall.

Five American presidents sought to prevent a communist Vietnam and possibly a communist Southeast Asia. Truman and Eisenhower provided mostly funds and equipment. When Kennedy became president there were fewer than one thousand U.S. advisers in Vietnam. By the time of his death in November 1963, there were sixteen thousand American troops in Vietnam. The Americanization of the war had begun.

Kennedy chose not to listen to the French president, Charles de Gaulle, who in May 1961 urged him to disengage from Vietnam, warning, "I predict you will sink step by step into a bottomless military and political quagmire."[38]

A debate continues as to what Kennedy would have done in Vietnam if he had served two terms—widen America's role or begin a slow but steady withdrawal. We do know that throughout his presidency, Kennedy talked passionately about the need to defend "frontiers of freedom" everywhere. In September 1963, he said "what happens in Europe or Latin America or Africa directly affects the security of the people who live in this city." Speaking in Fort Worth, Texas, on the morning of November 22, the day he was assassinated, Kennedy said bluntly that "without the United States, South Viet-Nam would collapse overnight.... We are still the keystone in the arch of freedom."[39]

Kennedy's successor, Lyndon B. Johnson, was an ambitious, experienced politician who had served in both the House and the Senate as a Democrat from Texas, and his persona was as large as his home state. He idolized FDR for winning World War II and initiating the New Deal and sought to emulate him as president. Like the three presidents who had preceded him, he saw action in time of war, serving as a naval aide in the Pacific during World War II, and like them he was a Christian, joining the Disciples of Christ Church in part for its focus on good works. Drawing on his political experience, Johnson thought that Ho Chi Minh was just another politician with whom he could bargain—offering a carrot or wielding a stick—just as he had done as the Senate majority leader. Ho Chi Minh, however, was not a backroom pol from Chicago or Austin but a communist revolutionary prepared to fight a protracted conflict and to accept enormous losses until he achieved victory.

Campaigning in 1964, Johnson promised, "We're not about to send American boys nine or ten thousand miles from home to do what Asian boys ought to be doing for themselves."[40] It was a promise he failed to honor. In August of that year, after North Vietnamese patrol boats reportedly attacked two U.S. destroyers, the president got the congressional authority he needed to increase the

American presence in Vietnam—the Gulf of Tonkin Resolution, passed by an overwhelming margin in the Senate.

Once elected, Johnson steadily increased the troop levels until by early 1968 there were more than half a million American servicemen in Vietnam—a course of action Eisenhower had strongly opposed. Johnson quadrupled the number of bombing raids against North Vietnam but barred any invasion of the North by U.S. or South Vietnamese forces, fearful of triggering a military response from Communist China. Johnson's fears were misplaced: China was caught up in the bloody chaos of the Cultural Revolution. For a decade, the People's Liberation Army was busy trying to advance the Cultural Revolution while controlling the Red Guards, the fanatical youth movement that the Cultural Revolution had unleashed.

Why was LBJ so determined to defend South Vietnam? Ever conscious of his place in history, the president compared the risk of Vietnam going communist to the "loss" of China in 1949: "I am not going to lose Vietnam," he vowed. "I am not going to be the president who saw Southeast Asia go the way China went."[41] In a nationally televised speech in 1965, he said, "The central lesson of our time is that the appetite of aggression is never satisfied. To withdraw from one battlefield means only to prepare for the next."[42]

But what if the enemy shows no sign of giving in? By 1968, after three and a half years of carefully calibrated escalation, the Pentagon concluded that the North Vietnamese could continue to send at least two hundred thousand men a year into South Vietnam indefinitely. As one analyst wrote, "The notion that we can 'win' this war by driving the VC-NVA [Viet-Cong and North Vietnamese Army] from the country or by inflicting an unacceptable rate of casualties on them is false."[43]

The Tet offensive of January 1968 seemed to confirm such an analysis. Some eighty-five thousand Viet Cong attacked Saigon and other major cities in the south. In most cases, the military historian Norman Friedman writes, the attackers achieved complete tactical surprise. There were dramatic successes, such as penetration of the U.S. embassy in Saigon and the capture of the old imperial capital Hue. Nevertheless, both the U.S. army and the South Vietnamese army fought well. The civilian population in the South did not rise up against the Saigon government but rejected the communist invaders. It was estimated that 40 percent of the communist cadres were killed or immobilized. The Viet Cong never recovered.

But the American news media reported the Tet offensive as a U.S. defeat, even a debacle. A frustrated and discouraged President Johnson did not know what to believe—the positive reports of his generals or the negative reporting of the media. The public opted for the latter.

Domestic opposition to the war was fueled by the mounting casualties (more than fifty-eight thousand Americans died in Vietnam). CBS News anchorman Walter Cronkite—the "most trusted man in America," according to a Gallup poll at the time—counseled America's withdrawal in a widely viewed telecast. The president is said to have told an aide that if they had "lost" Cronkite, they had lost the average citizen.[44] Tens and then hundreds of thousands of anti-war protestors filled the streets of Washington, D.C., chanting, "Hey, hey, LBJ, how many kids did you kill today?"

The inability of the United States to achieve a "final" military victory over the North Vietnamese seemed to confirm Mao's axiom that peasant armies could triumph over modern armies if they were patient and had the necessary will—qualities North Vietnam had in abundance.

Furthermore, the war in Vietnam was affecting U.S. strategic planning across the board. By 1968, experts argued, it would be difficult for the United States to respond anywhere else in the world because of its commitments in Vietnam.

FOUR

DÉTENTE
(1969-1980)

I n October 1964, Leonid Brezhnev, the ultimate appa-
ratchik, replaced the unpredictable Nikita Khrushchev
as the general secretary of the Communist Party of the
Soviet Union. Stalinist members of the Politburo had
never forgiven Khrushchev for his anti-Stalin speech at
the Twentieth Party Congress, and an overly confident
Khrushchev had failed to deliver on his promises to
improve the Soviet economy. Brezhnev kept his promise
to the Soviet military—when Lyndon Johnson left the
White House in January 1969, Moscow was close to
parity with the United States in land-based intercontinental ballistic missiles.[1]

Emulating the Stalinist cult of personality, Brezhnev instituted a policy of calculated oppression. Rather than sending all dissidents to the Gulag (which still existed), Brezhnev's KGB more often fired them from their jobs and expelled them from the Communist Party, rendering them powerless and destitute. It also began placing the more outspoken dissidents in psychiatric hospitals, where they were given electric shock treatment and mind-altering drugs.[2]

One victim of this treatment was Vladimir Bukovsky, who was "diagnosed" with various mental illnesses because he had engaged in political dissent. Here is an excerpt from his bestselling memoir, *To Build a Castle*:

> You are alone in the punishment cell, in the box. There, you get no paper, no pencil, and no books.... You get fed only every other day.... Blankets or warm clothes are forbidden.... Dried gobs of bloody saliva adorn the walls from the TB sufferers who have been incarcerated here before you.... At night you can doze off for only ten to fifteen minutes at a time before leaping up again and running in place...to get yourself

warm.... Three times a day they bring you a
drink of water.... Time comes to a halt.... Gradually the patches on the walls start to weave
themselves into faces as if the entire cell were
adorned with the portraits of prisoners who have
been here before you—it is a picture gallery of
all your predecessors.[3]

The Soviets also acted decisively to preserve communist
solidarity in Eastern and Central Europe. In 1967, Alexander Dubcek, the new communist party leader of Czechoslovakia, decided to institute a Khrushchev-like thaw, the
so-called "socialism with a human face." Neither the Soviets nor the hard-liners in their satellites wanted any such
experiment. Brezhnev considered a military solution as
early as April 1968. Directed by the Kremlin, the armed
forces of the Warsaw Pact, except for Romania, poured
into Czechoslovakia in August, ending the "Prague Spring."
Dubcek was summarily removed from office and later
forced to resign as first secretary of the Communist Party.

At a post-invasion meeting with Warsaw Pact leaders,
Brezhnev boasted that victory in the Cold War was in
sight—within two decades the United States would be

beaten. And he proclaimed a new doctrine: each socialist country, and especially the Soviet Union, had a duty not only to preserve socialism at home but protect it abroad—by force if necessary. In fact, the Brezhnev Doctrine was not new but a corollary of the Leninist Doctrine that power once acquired is never relinquished, either internally or externally.[4]

Brezhnev's embrace of "peaceful coexistence" was cynical in the extreme. The Kremlin regarded peaceful coexistence as a strategy of avoiding outright war with the United States while making the world socialist. It was a strategy formulated by Lenin, who called peaceful coexistence "the (temporary) absence of armed hostilities" while awaiting the "inevitable" world revolution. By 1970, the term had been redefined as "the intensification of the international class struggle," especially in the Third World.[5] Even as he was signing the first Strategic Arms Limitations Treaty (SALT I) in 1972, Brezhnev told party leaders that "the world outlook and class aims of socialism and capitalism are opposite and irreconcilable."[6]

At a dinner for Fidel Castro in June 1972, Brezhnev drove home the point regarding the role of peaceful coexistence:

While pressing for the assertion of the principle of peaceful coexistence, we realize that successes in this important matter in no way signify the possibility of weakening our ideological struggle. On the contrary, we should be prepared for an intensification of this struggle and for its becoming an increasingly acute form of struggle between the two social systems.[7]

Meanwhile, U.S. leaders from Richard Nixon to Gerald Ford to Jimmy Carter raised high the banner of "détente," defined by them as a relaxation or reduction of tensions between Western and communist nations. The Soviets were happy to toast détente while communizing nations wherever they could. A weary America regarded détente as a way for each side to show restraint in its relations with the other, while the Soviet Union, ever aggressive, understood détente to be a continuing competitive relationship arising from ideological, economic, and strategic incompatibility.

NIXON, KISSINGER, AND DÉTENTE

By the time of the Nixon presidency, the nature of the Cold War had changed. Applying its interpretation of peaceful coexistence, an aggressive Soviet Union called for "wars of national liberation," and supported many of them in the 1960s.

The communist world had grown substantially, spreading from Eastern Europe, China, North Korea, and North Vietnam to other parts of Asia (Cambodia and Afghanistan), Africa (Angola and Mozambique), and Latin America (Nicaragua). Many political and intellectual elites in industrialized countries openly voiced their preference for the policies of Moscow and Beijing rather than Washington and London. The nonaligned world, led by India, often sided with the communist bloc in the United Nations and regional organizations, while presenting itself as neutral.

The American domestic scene had also substantially changed. After twenty years, the bipartisan consensus on the Cold War was coming apart. Anti-war demonstrations were increasing, and congressional hawks were turning into doves. Vietnam was a major, but not the only, cause of contention. So was the issue of nuclear parity.

The Soviet Union had made quick progress building its nuclear program, while the United States chose to permit parity through defense spending decisions and arms control treaties. Supporters of the parity policy argued that the decision was forced by limited means and a balancing of defense and domestic needs. Opponents countered that America should have fought the Vietnam War differently and made different decisions regarding national security and domestic priorities. They stressed that the United States should have pursued a policy of peace through strength rather than peace through negotiations from a position of parity.

A leading advocate for staying true to Trumanesque containment was the liberal Democratic Senator Henry Jackson of Washington, who told a foreign affairs conference in March 1968, "We have heard a good deal of talk about détente, but I have the uncomfortable feeling that this talk says more about the state of mind in the West than about Soviet ambition and policy toward Western Europe."[8] Jackson admired Truman's inner toughness, compassion, and ability to make decisions, calling him "the architect of containment and the building of Europe that prevented the Russians from dominating Europe."[9]

Despite his Quaker roots, Nixon had a reputation as a staunch anticommunist, having come to national prominence as a Republican member of the House Un-American Activities Committee investigating the Alger Hiss case.

Before representing California in both the House and Senate, he had served as a navy lieutenant commander in the Pacific during World War II. As an active and trusted vice president under Eisenhower, he developed a keen interest in foreign policy.

Campaigning for the presidency in the fall of 1968, Nixon said that the United States should "seek a negotiated end to the war" in Vietnam while insisting that "the right of self-determination of the South Vietnamese people" had to be respected by all nations, including North Vietnam. Pressed for details, Nixon said he had "a secret plan" that he would reveal after he was elected. It turned out to be "Vietnamization," the turning over of the ground fighting to South Vietnamese forces, backed by U.S. air power.

Nixon and Henry Kissinger (first as national security adviser and then secretary of state) agreed on the need to accept the world as it was—conflicted and competitive—and to make the most of it. It was in America's interest, Kissinger said, to encourage a multipolar world and move toward a new world order based on "mutual restraint, coexistence, and ultimately cooperation."[10]

Containing communism was no longer U.S. policy, as it had been under the previous four administrations.

In a multipolar world—comprising the United States, the Soviet Union, China, Europe, and Japan—America could work even with communist countries as long as they promoted global stability, the new core of U.S. foreign policy.

The Nixon Doctrine contained three parts:

1. The United States would honor existing treaty commitments;
2. It would provide a nuclear shield to any ally or nation vital to U.S. security;
3. It would furnish military and economic assistance but not manpower to a nation considered important but not vital to the national interest.

Gone was the Truman-Eisenhower-Kennedy understanding that a loss of freedom anywhere was a loss of freedom everywhere. As Kissinger put it, "Our interests shall shape our commitments rather than the other way around."[11]

Nixon was most lucid about his foreign policy strategy in his June 1974 commencement speech at the U.S. Naval Academy. He suggested that U.S. foreign policy should be guided by a fusion of idealism and realism. But the president spent much of his speech on what he really thought was important: making his kind of realism the basis for American foreign policy in general and Cold War policy in particular. Because there were limits to what America could achieve and because U.S. actions might produce a slowdown or even reversal of détente, Nixon rejected the notion that the United States should aim to transform the internal behavior of other states.

"We would not welcome the intervention of other countries in our domestic affairs," Nixon said, "and we cannot expect them to be cooperative when we seek to intervene directly in theirs." At the same time, he emphasized that the goal of peace between nations with totally different systems was also a high moral objective. Nixon's eye was on building and sustaining a relative peace and stability among the great powers in which the status of the United States could be preserved.[12]

The Nixon-Kissinger foreign policy team went to work, beginning with Vietnam. In four years, the Nixon administration reduced American forces in Vietnam from 550,000 to twenty-four thousand. Spending dropped from twenty-five billion dollars a year to less than three billion. In 1972, the president abolished the draft, eliminating a primary issue of the anti-war protestors. At the same time, he kept up the American bombing in North Vietnam and added targets in Cambodia and Laos that were being used by Vietcong forces as sanctuaries, while seeking a negotiated end to the war.

An impatient Congress and public pressed the administration for swifter results and accurate accounts of the war. President Johnson and Secretary of Defense Robert McNamara had been guilty of making egregiously false claims about gains and losses in Vietnam.

When North Vietnam continued to use Cambodia as a staging ground for forays into South Vietnam, Nixon approved a Cambodian incursion in May 1970 by U.S. and Vietnamese troops. Escalation of the war produced widespread student protests, including a tragic confrontation at Kent State University, where four students were killed by inexperienced members of the Ohio National Guard. On June 24, the Senate decisively repealed the 1964 Gulf of Tonkin Resolution, which had first authorized the use of U.S. force in Vietnam. It later passed the Cooper-Church Amendment prohibiting the use of American ground troops in Laos or Cambodia.

Nixon tried to exploit the open differences between the Soviet Union and Communist China, reflected in the armed clashes in March 1969 along the Sino-Soviet border. Nixon warned the Kremlin secretly that the United States would not take lightly any Soviet attack on China. He and Kissinger initiated secret negotiations with China that resulted in Nixon's historic visit in February 1972. Mao Zedong and China's premier, Zhou Enlai, led Nixon to believe they would encourage North Vietnam to end the conflict. Conservatives criticized Nixon's unofficial "recognition" of Communist China because it weakened U.S. relations with the Republic of China on Taiwan, which functioned as a political alternative to the mainland and also served as a forward base for the U.S. military in Southeast Asia.

While the diplomatic talks between Washington and Beijing were proceeding, critics pointed out that Mao had plunged China into a virtual civil war known as the Great Proletarian Cultural Revolution. Seeking to destroy the Four Old-Fashioned Things—old ideas, old culture, old customs, and old habits—the aging revolutionary used the extremist Red Guards to pit the youth against the elderly, family members against each other, and countryside against city, declaring, "We don't want gentleness, we want war." As the social scientist Paul Hollander writes, the Cultural

Revolution degenerated into "political witch hunts and orgies of public violence."[13] Spurred on by Mao, the Red Guards attacked anyone they considered to be "insufficiently revolutionary." At last Mao was obliged to turn to the People's Liberation Army to subdue the Red Guards, who had begun targeting Communist Party officials. As many as one million Chinese died.[14] In Adam Ulam's words, "the Cultural Revolution revealed the irrationality lurking beneath Communist ideology and practice."[15]

On January 22, 1973, in Paris, Secretary of State William Rogers and North Vietnam's chief negotiator, Le Duc Tho, signed "An Agreement on Ending the War and Restoring Peace in Vietnam." In announcing the ceasefire, Nixon said five times that it represented the "peace with honor" he had promised since the 1968 presidential campaign. But the United States accepted North Vietnam's most crucial demand—that its troops be allowed to stay in the South—a concession that sealed the fate of South Vietnam. It hardly mattered that the United States could maintain aircraft carriers in South Vietnamese waters and use planes based in Taiwan and Thailand if Hanoi broke the accords. Airpower hadn't won the war. It wouldn't secure the peace.

The North Vietnamese began violating the peace treaty as soon as it was signed, moving men and equipment into South Vietnam to rebuild their almost decimated forces. In response, the United States provided modest military aid to South Vietnam and bombed North Vietnamese bases in Cambodia. The only tangible result was that in August 1973 an angry Congress cut off the funds for such bombing. In November 1973, it passed a War Powers Resolution requiring the president to inform Congress within forty-eight hours of any overseas deployment of U.S. forces and to bring the troops home within sixty days unless Congress expressly approved the president's action.

It is possible, although doubtful, that Nixon and Kissinger might have come up with a scheme to extend aid to the beleaguered South Vietnamese, but the Watergate scandal engulfed the Nixon White House. The president was preoccupied with his own survival, not South Vietnam's. He acknowledged his personal defeat in August 1974, resigning as president—the first president in U.S. history to do so—rather than suffer certain impeachment and conviction.

In January 1975 North Vietnam launched a general invasion, and one million refugees fled from central South

Vietnam toward Saigon. The new president, Gerald R. Ford, asked Congress for emergency assistance to "allies fighting for their lives." An obdurate Congress declined. On April 21, South Vietnamese President Nguyen Van Thieu and his government resigned. Ten days later, North Vietnamese forces took Saigon, and Marine helicopters lifted American officials and a few Vietnamese allies from the rooftop of the U.S. embassy, "an image of flight and humiliation etched on the memories of countless Americans," in the words of the British historian Paul Johnson.[16] Hanoi raised its flag on May 1 and renamed the old capital Ho Chi Minh City. South Vietnam was no more.

But the dominoes had only begun to fall. In mid-April, the communist Khmer Rouge entered the Cambodian capital of Phnom Penh. Their objective was to carry out in just one year the revolutionary changes that had taken more than a quarter-century in Mao's China. Between April 1975 and the beginning of 1977, the Marxist-Leninists ruling Cambodia killed an estimated 1.5 million people, one-fifth of the population. Widespread atrocities also took place in Laos, which remains under communist rule to this day.

Proportionally, the Cambodian massacre was the worst mass killing of the twentieth century, surpassing those of the Soviet Union, Nazi Germany, and Communist China. The principal architect of the "Killing Fields" of Cambodia was Pol Pot, who developed his genocidal brand of Maoism studying in Paris. Pol Pot was too much even for other communists like Vietnam's Ha Van Lau, who charged that Pot had transformed Cambodia into a "living hell" of massacres, forced labor, famine, and human degradation.[17]

Paul Johnson drew this appalling picture of Phnom Penh on the day the Khmer Rouge began to carry out their "social revolution" by emptying the city of three million people.

> The first killings came at 8:45 a.m. An hour later they opened fire on anyone seen in the streets. At noon hundreds of sick men, women and children were driven out of hospitals. All papers and records were destroyed. All books were thrown into the Mekong River. Cars, motorbikes, and bicycles were impounded. Rockets and bazookas were fired at houses where any movement was detected. By evening, the water-supply was cut off. By June, 3.5 million people from the cities

and 500,000 from "bad" villages had been scattered over the countryside.[18]

The 1973 Arab-Israeli war (the Yom Kippur War), in
which the Soviet Union openly supported Syria and
Egypt with a massive sea and air lift of arms and supplies, also set back détente. When the Israelis turned the
tide and came close to destroying Egyptian forces along
the Suez Canal, Brezhnev threatened to intervene. Nixon
put the U.S. military on worldwide alert, causing the
Soviets to back off and agree to a ceasefire that included
a UN emergency contingent.

THE FAILURE OF DÉTENTE

Détente peaked in 1975, the year of the Helsinki
Accords between the Soviet bloc and the West, and died
in 1979, the year of the USSR's invasion of Afghanistan.
At Helsinki, the West accepted the Soviet-imposed border
changes from the end of World War II and agreed to
increase trade with the Soviet Union, whose economy
was lagging badly behind those of Western nations. In
exchange, the Soviets and their satellites agreed to respect
human rights within their borders.

This did not seem to be a significant Soviet concession. The communist parties of the Soviet bloc were
apparently in firm control—the brutal suppression of the
1968 Prague Spring was still fresh in people's minds—
and the West did not seem interested in allowing human
rights to interfere with détente.

But human rights advocates within the Soviet Union
and Eastern and Central Europe used the Helsinki
accords to challenge the old communist order. They laid
the foundation for the people's revolution that brought
about the collapse of communism a little more than a
decade later.

Helsinki's considerable impact inside the Soviet Union
was unexpected. Anatoly Dobrynin, the Soviet ambassador to the United States from 1962 to 1986, wrote that
Brezhnev thought it would not cause "any trouble" inside
Soviet Russia, "but he was wrong." While the condition
of Soviet dissidents did not change overnight, they were
"definitely encouraged by this historic document.... It
gradually became a manifesto of the dissident...move-
ment."[19] By the summer of 1976, a Public Group to Promote Observance of the Helsinki Accords was operating
in Moscow with the blessing of Andrei Sakharov, the

Russian nuclear physicist who became a renowned human rights advocate. Similar "Helsinki Groups," including Václav Havel's Charter 77 group in Czechoslovakia, were appearing all over Eastern and Central Europe.

No sign of cataclysmic change was visible in the early 1970s, but by the end of the decade, it was clear that détente had failed as a substitute for the policy of containment. John Lewis Gaddis has identified several reasons for this failure. Nixon and Kissinger had attempted to link benefits like Western exports of food and technology to the peaceful advancement of Soviet interests in the Third World, but linkage had not produced the results promised. Had Soviet behavior actually changed? The Soviets accepted the 1973 Egyptian surprise attack on Israel, provided aid to communists in Portugal following a 1974 revolution, did nothing in 1975 to keep North Vietnam from overrunning South Vietnam, and used Cuban troops as proxies in 1974 to install a Marxist government in Angola. Furthermore, during the Ford and Carter administrations the Soviets supported Marxist regimes in Somalia and Ethiopia, exploited Marxist coups in South Yemen and Afghanistan, and in 1979 invaded Afghanistan. They armed and trained revolutionaries in at least twenty-five countries, including Angola, Mozambique, Nicaragua, Uruguay, and Mexico.[20]

It did not occur to the apostles of détente, apparently, that the Soviets were more interested in furthering socialism in the Third World than in preserving stability. For the Soviets, détente did not mean an end to U.S.-Soviet competition but only an agreement not to escalate the competition to dangerous levels.[21] Proud of their realist theory, Nixon and Kissinger (and their immediate successors) chose not to see that the Soviets had not abandoned the ideological goal of global socialism.

Détente also papered over Communist China's totalitarian behavior behind the Bamboo Curtain. During this period, millions of Chinese (and Tibetans) died at the hands of the ruling Communist Party and the PLA while the cult of Mao the "Great Helmsman" was enhanced both inside and outside China. Nixon and Kissinger insisted that China, like the Soviet Union, should not be judged by the usual humanitarian standards. Détente, they argued, was more important than what governments said and did to their own people, no matter how reprehensible their behavior. Détente advanced China's international standing at the expense of the Republic of China and non-communist Chinese throughout Asia.

Caught up in its own rhetoric, the White House encouraged Congress and the public to expect too much from linkage. At their May 1972 summit, Nixon and Brezhnev signed a statement of "Basic Principles" governing U.S.-Soviet relations in which the two powers promised that they would avoid military confrontation and exercise restraint. The statement set an unrealistically high standard the Soviets had no intention of meeting, as their aggressive actions throughout the 1970s demonstrated. Yet Kissinger continued to postulate that the Soviet Union would find it in its interest to practice "self-containment."

While depending heavily on linkage, the Nixon-Ford-Kissinger triumvirate made the most substantial reductions in America's national defense in the postwar period. Defense spending as a percentage of gross domestic product went from 8.2 percent in fiscal year 1970 to 5.2 percent in fiscal year 1977. The Soviets were spending several times as much of their GDP on their military arsenal. Kissinger was seemingly resigned to the growth of Soviet military strength. His goal was strategic parity (not superiority) between the Soviet Union and the United States as a path to global stability.

The second failure of détente was arms control agreements with the Soviets. SALT I was meant to be the centerpiece of arms control. The treaty limited the Soviet military buildup without restricting future steps the United States might take to upgrade its strategic arms. One important disadvantage was that it froze Soviet missile strength at a much higher level than the U.S. arsenal—1330 Soviet ICBMs versus 1054 American ICBMs.

SALT I was soon rendered obsolete by the continuing arms race. Both sides took advantage of their right to modernize and increased the number of their strategic warheads. In an attempt to slow down the arms race, President Carter, after taking office in 1977, further cut the defense budget. The Soviets responded by continuing their buildup of nuclear and conventional weapons.

The Soviets increased concern among U.S. allies by deploying a new generation of mobile intermediate-range missiles (the SS-20) in Eastern Europe; the SS-20 had an initial maximum range of 3,100 miles, threatening all of Western Europe. When the Interim SALT I agreement expired in 1977, both sides were more heavily armed than before. But for the first time since 1945, the United States no longer had overall military superiority.

A third failure of Nixon-Kissinger-style détente was its focus on great power politics to the neglect of the rest of the world. American foreign policy was insensitive to local concerns such as the rise of anti-colonialism in Angola and Mozambique, focusing instead on how Moscow or Beijing might react to U.S. policy.

Both the Left and the Right charged that Nixon and Kissinger were more attracted to global stability than human rights. Liberals pointed to U.S. relations with authoritarian regimes in South Korea, the Philippines, Pakistan, Iran, Greece, Portugal, and Chile. Conservatives complained about the administration's silence about communist suppression in the Soviet Union, Eastern and Central Europe, Cuba, and China. In 1973 a congressional coalition of anti-communist liberals and conservatives forced the State Department to submit annual reports on the state of human rights in more than one hundred countries.

Kissinger argued that given the hand he was dealt— the public's weariness with the protracted nature of the Cold War and Congress's hostility to the Vietnam War and similar acts of military "adventurism"—balance-of-power détente was the best possible policy. But Kissinger was never able to build a widespread public consensus for his foreign policy. His efforts were weakened by the inability of the two presidents he served to help him. The beleaguered Nixon was too busy coping with Watergate, and the inarticulate Ford was incapable of explaining détente to a public wary of Washington rhetoric.

JIMMY CARTER

Jimmy Carter faced much the same world as Nixon had but tried a far different approach to the Cold War. Although a graduate of the U.S. Naval Academy who had served for six years after World War II, he was equally or even more formed by his evangelical Baptist faith, his family roots in Plains, Georgia, his background as a peanut farmer, and his political experiences as a Southern and Democratic governor. In his inaugural address, Carter promised to marshal "our forces" against poverty, ignorance, and injustice and to build "a lasting peace, based not on our weapons of war but on international policies which reflect our own most precious values." He even attempted to bypass the Cold War, declaring in a speech at the University of Notre Dame in May 1977 that the democratic West was now free of an "inordinate fear of communism."[22]

Carter thought the stalemate of the Cold War could be overridden by focusing on world order issues. He did not seem to believe, at least at the beginning of his presidency, that the Cold War was still the primary issue in world politics.

In his first news conference, he announced his intention to withdraw U.S. ground troops from South Korea, a decision he was later forced to rescind. In December 1978, he established formal diplomatic relations with the People's Republic of China and unilaterally severed relations with the Republic of China in Taiwan, a U.S. ally since World War II.

Critics like former Congressman Walter Judd asserted that Carter's executive decision (made without congressional approval) was not only morally but politically wrong because other allies would now wonder "how dependable are our commitments to them." It was diplomatically wrong because mainland China would not accept such an arrangement as final. It was economically wrong because it jeopardized America's profitable two-way trade with Taiwan. Congress agreed with Judd's blunt criticism and in April 1979, led by liberal Democrats such as Clement Zablocki in the House and Frank Church in the Senate, passed the Taiwan Relations Act, which pledged the U.S. government to preserve and promote "extensive, close and friendly commercial and cultural contacts" with Taiwan. The United States was also required to make available weapons that would enable Taiwan to "maintain a sufficient self-defense capability." Furthermore, the president was obliged to promptly inform Congress "of any threat to the security or the social or economic system" of Taiwan and to take "appropriate action" in response to "any such danger." The act was a stinging rebuff to Carter, who signed it without a public word.[23]

Amid the sharp debate between the executive and legislative branches of government, Senator Barry Goldwater, a Republican from Arizona, led a legal challenge against the president, arguing that the Senate or both houses of Congress should give approval before the United States abrogated any of the post–World War II mutual defense treaties. His position was affirmed when the Senate voted unanimously that the president should not nullify a treaty without first seeking the advice and consent of the Senate. A determined Goldwater brought suit in federal court against Carter to prevent him from terminating the Taiwan defense treaty unless Congress approved. The senator prevailed in the U.S. district court, but the decision was reversed on appeal. In December 1979 the Supreme Court declined to hear the case.

Although unsuccessful, Goldwater's legal challenge affected U.S. policy in three important ways. It signaled that Congress was not content to be merely a junior partner in the making of foreign policy, it reminded the executive branch that the principle of checks and balances applied to foreign as well as domestic affairs, and it strengthened the determination of Congress to pass the strongest possible Taiwan Relations Act.[24]

Carter continued to press for a SALT II throughout his administration, even though Soviet violations of SALT I were widely suspected and Soviet violations of human rights were well known. His attachment to SALT II reflected his conviction that no issue was more important than the threat of nuclear annihilation. He placed human rights and the fear of nuclear weapons at the center of his world view—not perceiving that he was creating an ultimately incompatible relationship and even violating the human rights of those behind the Iron and Bamboo Curtains.

Carter envisioned a world order shaped by self-determination, global diplomacy and international organizations, and a concern with human rights. "We can no longer separate the traditional issues of war and peace," he said at Notre Dame, "from the new global questions of justice, equity, and human rights." For Carter, the Cold War was just one of several especially challenging problems, such as race, wealth, and regional conflicts, that had to be faced and solved.[25]

While granting that the Soviets remained a military threat, the president did not accept that communist movements in the Third World were a threat or were part of any global communist conspiracy. The overriding Third World issue, he declared, was poverty, not ideology. Détente remained the keystone of U.S. foreign policy until the Soviet invasion of Afghanistan in December 1979. Secretary of State Cyrus Vance happily complied with Carter's instructions and blocked any attempt to link Soviet aggressiveness in the Third World with U.S.-Soviet relations.

For the president, the Cold War was basically limited to Europe. Like President Kennedy fifteen years before, Carter wanted NATO to stand up to the Soviets but without relying on nuclear weapons. That could be done, he asserted, if every member country increased its defense spending by 3 percent each year. Accustomed to sheltering under the American nuclear umbrella for protection

Lenin's Dream." (National Archives)

Prime Minister Winston Churchill, President Franklin D. Roosevelt, and Soviet leader Joseph Stalin at the Yalta summit, February 1945. (National Archives)

Churchill and FDR at Yalta. (Copyright Unknown, Courtesy of Harry S. Truman Library)

Prime Minister Churchill, President Harry S. Truman, and Soviet leader Joseph Stalin at the Potsdam conference, July 1945. (U.S. Army Signal Corps, Courtesy of Harry S. Truman Library)

Foreign ministers of the Big Three and their aides at Potsdam. (U.S. Navy, Courtesy of Harry S. Truman Library)

President Truman at Winston Churchill's
Iron Curtain speech, March 5, 1946.
(Terry Savage, Courtesy of Harry S. Truman Library)

Loading supply planes for the Berlin Airlift, 1948.
(Byers, Joint Export Import Agency, Courtesy of Harry S. Truman
Library)

Planes prepare for
takeoff as part of the
Berlin Airlift.
(Copyright Unknown,
Courtesy of Harry S. Truman
Library)

Mao Zedong addresses the crowd at the beginning of the People's Republic of China, circa 1950. (Public Domain)

Hungarian Freedom Fighters take on the Soviet army in the 1956 Hungarian Revolution. (Wikimedia Commons)

East German soldiers patrol the Berlin Wall, erected in 1961. (Public Domain)

Chairman Mao Zedong and President Richard Nixon in Beijing, February 1972. (National Archives)

Skulls taken from the mass grave of Choeung Ek in Cambodia's "Killing Fields," 1975–1979.

(Photo by Adam Jones adamjones.freeservers.com)

President Ronald Reagan and Soviet president Mikhail Gorbachev at the Reykjavik summit, October 1986. (Courtesy Ronald Reagan Library)

Reagan and Gorbachev take a break at Reykjavik. (Courtesy Ronald Reagan Library)

Reagan and Gorbachev walk away from Reykjavik. (Courtesy Ronald Reagan Library)

President Reagan at the Brandenburg Gate, Berlin, in June 1987: "Mr. Gorbachev, tear down this wall!" (Courtesy Ronald Reagan Library)

Reagan gives a "thumbs-up" at the Brandenburg Gate. (Courtesy Ronald Reagan Library)

Standing on top of a tank, Russian president Boris Yeltsin rallies people against the attempted Soviet coup, August 1991.

(Associated Press)

against Soviet aggression, NATO members declined to spend more.

In the spring of 1978, the Carter administration reviewed its foreign policy and decided to place more emphasis on arms control, although the national security adviser, Zbigniew Brzezinski, urged a strong national defense to counter Soviet power. Vance, however, was all for negotiation and détente.

Believing that arms control agreements should be sought regardless of Soviet behavior in other areas, Carter joined Brezhnev in signing SALT II in June 1979. The treaty sought to control strategic nuclear weapons by, among other things, reducing the delivery systems on both sides. Promising on paper, SALT II's implementation depended upon Moscow's keeping its promises. The uneasiness with which some experts viewed the treaty is reflected in the comment of a senior American diplomat that Carter ignored a fundamental rule in U.S.-Soviet relations: the American public wanted both negotiation and U.S. strength, not one or the other.[26] As we will see, President Reagan understood this American trait very well.

Carter thought that most of the world's problems flowed from the often antagonistic relationship between the developed North and the undeveloped South—often called the Third World. So he set about eliminating the causes of conflict. He negotiated a treaty turning over the Panama Canal to Panamanian control by the end of the century. He cut off U.S. support of the authoritarian Somoza regime in Nicaragua, enabling the Cuban-backed Sandinistas to overthrow Somoza and gain control of the government.

As part of its human rights campaign, the Carter administration advised the Iranian military not to suppress accelerating pro-Islamic demonstrations and riots. The shah of Iran, the chief U.S. ally in the region, was soon in exile. Encouraged by the Ayatollah Khomeini, the de facto leader of the country, militant Iranians paraded through the streets calling America the "great Satan." They seized the U.S. embassy in Teheran and held fifty-two Americans as hostages for fourteen and a half months.

Carter made the mistake of admitting publicly that he felt the same helplessness that a powerful person feels when his child is kidnapped. As the political scientist Michael Kort points out, the admission made the United States look like "a weak and helpless giant as the Iranians mistreated the hostages and taunted the president." A failed rescue attempt in April 1980 only made the United States and the president look weaker. Not until the eve of Carter's leaving office in January 1980 (after having been defeated for reelection) did Iran release the hostages. "By then," writes Kort, "Carter's foreign policy and his presidency lay in ruins."[27]

The renowned scholar of foreign affairs Jeane Kirkpatrick (later the U.S. ambassador to the United Nations under Reagan) thought that Carter's pivotal mistake was his failure to distinguish between the relative danger of totalitarian and authoritarian regimes. Carter did not perceive that the shah of Iran and Nicaragua's Somoza were less dangerous to U.S. interests than the fundamentalist Muslim and Marxist regimes that replaced them. In her definitive 1979 essay, "Dictatorships and Double Standards," Kirkpatrick wrote:

> The foreign policy of the Carter administration failed not for lack of good intentions but for lack of realism about the nature of traditional versus revolutionary autocracies and the relation of each to the American national interest.... [T]raditional authoritarian governments are less repressive than revolutionary autocracies, are

more susceptible of liberalization, and they are more compatible with U.S. interests.[28]

Beyond "reasonable" doubt, she wrote, the communist governments of Vietnam, Cambodia, and Laos were much more repressive that those of "despised previous rulers." The government of the People's Republic of China was more repressive than that of Taiwan; North Korea was more repressive than South Korea. "Traditional autocrats," she wrote, "tolerate social inequities, brutality, and poverty, whereas revolutionary autocracies create them."[29]

President Carter's single major accomplishment in foreign policy came in 1978 when he brought Prime Minister Menachem Begin of Israel and President Anwar Sadat of Egypt to the United States to negotiate and sign the Camp David Accords, which established peace between two old enemies and marked a significant shift in Arab resistance to Israel's right to exist. They were an historic achievement but had little impact on the Cold War.

AFGHANISTAN

After a string of notable foreign policy successes, the Soviets were about to encounter an unexpected setback.

In October 1979, Hafizulah Amin, a formerly reliable communist politician, engineered a coup in Afghanistan, ousting his pro-Moscow rival and provoking the Kremlin to intervene and establish a pro-Soviet government. On December 27, 1979, Soviet special forces killed Amin and replaced him with a Soviet puppet. The Soviet Union found itself directly involved in an Afghan civil war.

By the time the chastened Soviets withdrew in February 1989, they had suffered 13,826 dead and 49,985 wounded. Afghanistan was the Soviet Union's Vietnam, a quagmire from which it could not extricate itself for nearly a decade.[30]

Admitting after the Soviet invasion of Afghanistan that he had learned more about communism in one week than he had in a lifetime, Carter initiated a series of anti-Soviet actions. He justified his new hard-line policy by exaggerating Moscow's entry into Afghanistan as "the greatest threat to peace since the Second World War."[31] He withdrew the SALT II treaty from Senate consideration. He embargoed grain imports to the Soviet Union. He announced that the United States would boycott the 1980 Olympics in Moscow. But he still insisted that he supported détente, puzzling U.S. foreign policy experts and causing the Soviets to wonder what he meant.

In January 1980 the president suddenly proclaimed the Carter Doctrine: any attempt by an outside power to gain control of the Persian Gulf would be regarded as a "direct assault on the vital interests of the United States," to be repelled "by any means necessary, including military force." As one historian wrote, reports of the demise of containment "had been somewhat exaggerated."[32]

Having entered the White House with a grand strategy to transcend long-held American fears about communism and to end the Cold War, President Carter was caught up in what he called Soviet "expansionism." Defeated in the election of 1980 by the conservative Ronald Reagan, Carter left office with Soviet-American relations at their lowest ebb in a decade and the Cold War seemingly fated to last for years to come.[33]

FIVE

WINNING THE COLD WAR
(1981–1991)

onald Reagan would permanently change the global picture, which looked bleak when he took office in 1981. From martial law in Poland imposed by the communist regime and the Soviet invasion of Afghanistan to the Sandinista revolution in Nicaragua and communist rule in Mozambique and Angola, Soviet Premier Leonid Brezhnev claimed victories for Marxism-Leninism.

Within the free world, the Atlantic alliance was strained. To counter the deployment in the late 1970s of Soviet SS-20 intermediate-range nuclear missiles aimed at major European cities, NATO proposed a dual-track approach—negotiations to remove the missiles and the deployment of U.S. Pershing II and cruise missiles aimed at Soviet cities. The latter sparked a popular movement in Western Europe, aided and abetted by the Kremlin, to freeze NATO's deployment of nuclear weapons, and Western European governments wavered in their resolve to counter the Soviets, even on their own soil.

Reagan put the deployment of the Euromissiles at the center of his new foreign policy. He forged a close friendship with British Prime Minister Margaret Thatcher and sought the support of other Western European leaders, particularly Chancellor Helmut Kohl of West Germany.

Unlike the foreign policy realists who viewed all regimes through the same lens, Reagan placed regime differences at the heart of his understanding of the Cold War. With his modest Illinois roots and biblical Christian faith learned from his mother, he emerged as a screen star and a committed anticommunist, fighting communist efforts to take over the Hollywood trade unions in the postwar period. Poor eyesight kept him stateside with the army during World War II, but his varied experiences contributed to his appreciation of the need for military strength. Two terms as a Republican governor of California confirmed his conservative, pro-freedom political views.

Reagan considered communism to be a disease and regarded the Soviet government as illegitimate. Like Truman, he believed Soviet foreign policy to be offensive by its very nature, and he saw the world as engaged in an ideological struggle between communism and liberal democracy. But unlike Truman, he sought in the circumstances of the 1980s not merely to contain the USSR but to defeat it.

Reagan had endorsed the strategy and insights of NSC 68 shortly after that key document of the Truman administration was declassified and published in 1975, devoting several of his radio commentaries to it. Also in the 1970s, he called for reductions, not limitations, in U.S. and Soviet armaments through verifiable agreements.

He identified as central weaknesses of the Soviet bloc the denial of religious freedom and the inability to provide consumer goods. He stressed that Pope John Paul II's trip to Poland in 1979 revealed that communist atheism—ruthlessly imposed for decades—had failed to stop the people from believing in God. Reagan noted the pope's language—"Do not be afraid!"—and the size of the crowds at the masses that he celebrated in Krakow, Warsaw, and other Polish cities. In Krakow, the pope's home city, between two and three million people welcomed him, the largest public gathering in the nation's history.

In a 1979 radio commentary, Reagan remarked that the pope, in his final public appearance, had invited the people to bring forward several large crosses for his blessing. Suddenly there was movement among the multitude of young people before him. They began raising thousands and thousands of crosses, many of them homemade, for the pope's blessing. "These young people of Poland," Reagan said, "had been born and raised and spent their entire lives under communist atheism. Try to make a Polish joke out of that."[1]

All these policy positions formed a main theme of Reagan's 1980 presidential campaign: real peace would come through the military strength of the West along with its political and economic freedom. For Reagan, as for Truman, the gravest threat to the United States and the free world came from the Soviet Union, whose continuing imperialist designs on every continent demanded a new Cold War strategy.

REAGAN: "WE WIN, AND THEY LOSE"

The new conservative president summed up the aims of his foreign policy as "We win, and they lose." In his first presidential news conference, Reagan stunned official

Washington by denouncing the Soviet leadership as still dedicated to "world revolution and a one-world socialist-communist state." As he put it in his 1990 autobiography, "I decided we had to send as powerful a message as we could to the Russians that we weren't going to stand by anymore while they armed and financed terrorists and subverted democratic governments."[2]

The foreign policy establishment was appalled at such saber rattling. Because the Soviet Union was apparently economically strong and militarily powerful, many continued to argue that the only responsible policy was détente. After visiting Moscow in 1982, Harvard professor Arthur Schlesinger Jr. declared, "Those in the U.S. who think the Soviet Union is on the verge of economic and social collapse, ready with one small push to go over the brink, are…only kidding themselves."[3] Two years later, the establishment's favorite economist, John Kenneth Galbraith, following a prolonged visit to the Soviet Union, delivered a glowing appraisal of Soviet economics. "The Russian system succeeds," he said, "because in contrast to the Western industrial economies, it makes full use of its manpower…. The Soviet economy has made great national progress in recent years."[4] The following year, 1985, Mikhail Gorbachev took command of an almost bankrupt Soviet Union.

Reagan's greatest strength, John Lewis Gaddis says, was his ability to see beyond complexity to simplicity. He saw that "because détente perpetuated—and had been meant to perpetuate—the Cold War, only killing détente could end the Cold War."[5]

Based on intelligence reports and his own instincts, Reagan concluded that communism was in fact cracking and ready to crumble. He took personal charge of U.S. foreign policy. In his first year, the president chaired fifty-seven meetings of the National Security Council.[6]

The president went public with his bold diagnosis of the Soviet Union's systemic weakness in May 1982, declaring that the Soviet empire was "faltering because rigid centralized control has destroyed incentives for innovation, efficiency and individual achievement." A month later, speaking to the British Parliament in Westminster, Reagan said that the Soviet Union was gripped by a "great revolutionary crisis," famously predicting that "the march of freedom and democracy...will leave Marxism-Leninism on the ash-heap of history as it has left other tyrannies which stifle the freedom and muzzle the self-expression of the people."[7]

Like Truman before him, Reagan did not accept that America should accommodate the Kremlin, and he resurrected Truman's policy that the United States should negotiate with the Soviets only from a position of strength. Further, he recognized the fatal weakness in the Soviet Union: it was continually expanding its empire but was suffering from serious political, economic, and spiritual weakness at its core. The president aimed to exploit this weakness through the application of American political, economic, and military power in order to bring the Soviets to the negotiating table on terms favorable to America and its allies.

The president directed his top national security team—CIA Director William Casey, Defense Secretary Caspar Weinberger, National Security Adviser Richard Allen, Allen's successor William P. Clark, and the State Department's Lawrence Eagleburger—to develop a plan to end the Cold War by winning it. As a result, the Pentagon produced a defense guidance for resource and force planning with two new objectives: (1) "Reverse the geographic expansion of Soviet control and military presence throughout the world" and (2) "Encourage long-term political and military changes within the Soviet empire."[8]

Reagan's new strategy of changing rather than simply containing the Soviet Union was implemented through a series of national security decision directives over the next year:

- NSDD-32, written by Richard Pipes, a distinguished Russian historian on leave from Harvard University, declared that the United States would seek to "neutralize" Soviet control over Eastern Europe. It also authorized the use of covert action and other means to support anti-Soviet groups in the region, including the Solidarity trade union in Poland.
- NSDD-66, drafted by National Security Council aide Roger Robinson, stated that it was U.S. policy to disrupt the Soviet economy by attacking a "strategic triad" of critical resources—financial credits, high technology, and natural gas. The directive was tantamount to a secret declaration of economic war on the Soviet Union.
- NSDD-73, also written by Pipes, called for the United States to seek not coexistence with the Soviet system but a fundamental

change of the system—something that the containment guru George Kennan hadn't thought possible. The Reagan administration proved Kennan wrong with a multifaceted foreign policy that included a substantial increase in pro-freedom public diplomacy and a drive to hurt the Soviet economy by reducing the price of oil.

A subset of the strategy for defeating the USSR was the "Reagan Doctrine," a term coined by the columnist Charles Krauthammer, which departed from the previous policy of containment by seeking to oust communist regimes. It approved U.S. support of pro-freedom forces in Afghanistan, Nicaragua, Angola, and Cambodia. To his credit, President Carter had begun helping the anti-Soviet mujahideen in Afghanistan during his final months in office. But a key Reagan decision was to supply Stinger ground-to-air missiles, which the mujahideen promptly used to shoot down the Soviet helicopters that had kept them on the defensive for years.

In Latin America, the Sandinistas were not only establishing a Leninist state in Nicaragua but supporting communist guerrillas in El Salvador and elsewhere. The

Reagan administration directed the CIA to form an anti-Sandinista movement—the Contras—and asked Congress to approve funds for them.

Reagan never contemplated sending U.S. troops to Nicaragua. He believed that with sufficient military support and firm diplomatic negotiation, Nicaraguans could rid themselves of the Marxist regime. He was proved correct by the results of the democratic elections of February 1990, when the anti-Sandinista Violeta Chamorro decisively defeated the Sandinista *commandante* Daniel Ortega for president.

With people, funds, and weapons, the Reagan Doctrine pushed containment to its logical conclusion by helping those who wanted to win their freedom. The doctrine was part of Reagan's overarching strategy to pressure the Soviets at their political, economic, military, and moral weak spots, build up Western strength, and press for victories on key Cold War battlefields.

A TURNING POINT

Nineteen eighty-three was a critical year for Reagan and the course of the Cold War. In March, he told a group of evangelical ministers that the Soviets "are the focus of evil in this modern world" and the masters of "an evil empire."[9] In the same month, the president announced that development and deployment of a comprehensive anti-ballistic missile system would be his top military priority. "I call upon the scientific community in our country," he said, "those who gave us nuclear weapons, to turn their great talents now to the cause of mankind and world peace, to give us the means of rendering these nuclear weapons impotent and obsolete."[10] Reagan had long favored an alternative to the policy of mutual assured destruction (MAD), under which the United States and the Soviet Union each retained the nuclear capability to retaliate and destroy the other in the event of a nuclear attack. Reagan's defense secretary Caspar Weinberger called MAD a "mutual suicide pact."[11]

The Strategic Defense Initiative (SDI) was ridiculed as "Star Wars" by detractors, but Yuri Andropov, who had succeeded Brezhnev as leader of the USSR in 1982, took the initiative very seriously, calling it a "strike weapon" and a preparation for a U.S. nuclear attack. Moscow's intense opposition to SDI showed that Soviet scientists regarded SDI not as a pipe dream but a technological feat they could not match. A decade later General Makhmut Gareev, who headed the department of strategic analysis in the Soviet Ministry of Defense, revealed what he had told the Politburo, the ruling body of the

Soviet Union, in 1983: "Not only could we not defeat SDI, SDI defeated all our possible countermeasures."[12]

More than any other strategic action he took, the president's unwavering commitment to SDI convinced the Kremlin it could not afford a continuing arms race and led Gorbachev to sue for peace, ending the Cold War at the bargaining table and not on the battlefield.

In October 1983, Reagan dispatched two thousand American troops, along with military units from six Caribbean states, to the tiny island of Grenada to oust a Marxist regime that had recently seized power. It was the first time in nearly forty years of the Cold War that America had acted to restore democracy to a communist country. The allegedly sacrosanct Brezhnev Doctrine— once a communist state, always a communist state—was successfully challenged. Initially criticized for an "unnecessary" military action in Grenada, Reagan was widely praised after an enormous cache of arms was uncovered—enough to equip a force of ten thousand men with automatic rifles, machine guns, rocket launchers, anti-aircraft guns, howitzers, and cannon—along with armored vehicles and coastal patrol boats.

That same fall, despite Soviet-coordinated protests in the streets of London, Rome, Paris, and other European cities, the Reagan administration proceeded with the deployment of Pershing II and cruise missiles in Western Europe. The stakes were high. Six Western European countries—Great Britain, the Federal Republic of Germany, Italy, Belgium, Norway, and the Netherlands—had elections scheduled for that year. Had voters turned against deployment, the NATO alliance would have been seriously weakened. Instead, because the West presented a united front, every one of the pro-deployment governments won.

All the while, privately as well as publicly, the president expressed his willingness to sit down and talk with the Soviet leadership. But they kept dying on him—Brezhnev in 1982, Yuri Andropov in 1983, and an aged Konstantin Chernenko in 1984.

IRAN-CONTRA

The Iran-Contra "scandal," always highlighted by liberal historians in their account of the Reagan years, had its origins in two quite different impulses of the president. The first was humanitarian—to free a handful of American hostages held by terrorists in Lebanon. The second was strategic—to support the anticommunist resistance in Nicaragua. The affair also underscored the ever increasing influence of the National Security Council on the conduct of U.S. foreign policy.

Frustrated NSC staffers asked themselves how the United States could negotiate with terrorists when such talks contradicted the administration's stated policy of not dealing with terrorists or a state like Iran that supported terrorist groups. Both Secretary of State George Shultz and Secretary of Defense Caspar Weinberger adamantly opposed negotiations. But NSC staffers believed that "moderate" elements in Iran could facilitate the release of the hostages. Reagan wrote in his memoir that "it was the president's DUTY to get them home."[13]

And so at the end of 1985, Reagan decided to proceed with an Iranian initiative that involved the exchange of arms for the release of Americans. A year later, the administration was trying to contain a political crisis that some critics equated with Nixon's Watergate. In March 1987, the president conceded reluctantly in a nationally televised address that he had tried to trade arms for hostages. "I let my personal concern for the hostages spill over into the geopolitical strategy of reaching out to Iran."[14] The public made clear its rejection of the deal: Reagan's approval rating dropped twenty-one points in one month, to 46 percent.

The "Contra" half of the scandal began in the fall of 1982 when Congress passed the first Boland amendment, prohibiting the expenditure of funds to "overthrow" the government of Nicaragua. Arguing that the Contras did not intend to overthrow the government, the administration continued to fund the rebels until December 1984, when Congress denied any direct or indirect support by any U.S. intelligence agency to the Contras. At this point, the pro-Contra effort was shifted from the CIA to the NSC, which the administration contended was not an "intelligence" agency, under the direction of John Poindexter and his aide Oliver North.

Apparently with the approval of CIA Director William Casey, North diverted profits from arms sales to the Contras. Asked by Reagan to investigate the matter, Attorney General Edwin Meese III called the diversion of funds "a tremendous error that should never have been allowed to happen."[15] North, Poindexter, and others were indicted and convicted on charges stemming from Iran-Contra. But unlike Nixon, Reagan did not try to cover up the affair. Iran-Contra was concerned with public policy; Watergate was always about politics. Reagan approved arms for hostages to save American lives; Nixon tried to contain Watergate to save himself.

In November 1987, a select committee of the House and Senate concluded that the president had been shielded from knowledge and had been unaware of the funds diversion. The Republican minority said that the mistakes of the Iran-Contra affair had been "mistakes in judgment and nothing more. There was no constitutional crisis, no systematic disrespect for the 'internal rule of law,' no grand conspiracy."[16] Iran-Contra soon faded from the public's consciousness as most Americans decided that it was an exception and not the rule of the Reagan Doctrine.

GORBACHEV

In March 1985, Mikhail Gorbachev, a protégé of the late Soviet leader Yuri Andropov, became general secretary of the Communist Party of the Soviet Union. Gorbachev took command of a nation and an empire in crisis. The Soviet Union was a Potemkin village, not a mighty nation-state. Seventy years after the Bolshevik Revolution, economic growth was stagnant, collective farms were unable to feed the people, most factories did not meet their quotas, consumers lined up for blocks in Moscow and other cities for the bare necessities, and the war in Afghanistan dragged on with no end in sight to the fighting or the deaths of thousands of young Soviet soldiers. As reflected in the emergence of Solidarity in Poland and Charter 77 in Czechoslovakia, the peoples of Eastern and Central Europe were increasingly unwilling to accept Soviet rule passively.

And yet, driven by nationalist pride and Leninist ideology, the Soviet Union persisted in its goal of creating a world-class military establishment. The Soviet fleet was comparable in power and range to the U.S. Navy. The Soviet Union could boast of parity with the United States in strategic weapons systems. Abroad, the Soviets could point to Marxist takeovers in Ethiopia (1974), South Vietnam (1975), and Nicaragua (1979) and the Soviet invasion of Afghanistan and installation of a puppet regime (1979).

But the system was rotten at its core. Gorbachev himself noted the paradox of a system able to send rockets to Venus but incapable of producing high-quality domestic appliances. The Soviet Union, the world's biggest producer of steel and fuel, was in short supply of both. The energetic new chairman set about trying to rejuvenate socialism in the place where it had been born.

In December 1984, three months before he took office, Gorbachev reassured Communist Party officials that his goal was to ensure that the Soviet Union began the twenty-first century "in a manner worthy of a great power." In May 1986, under the rubric of *uskorenye* (acceleration), he tried to speed up socialism by improving the quality of goods, retooling industry, and even reducing alcoholism through central planning.

Uskorenye quickly ran out of gas, but a stubborn Gorbachev insisted, "We are not giving up on socialism; we want to make it better." The general secretary was never a capitalist in the making. As late as 1988, he quoted *The Communist Manifesto* when asked his position on private property.[17]

His reforms, widely hailed in the West, were always intended to stabilize and then strengthen the Soviet regime. He next sought reform at the top through *perestroika* (restructuring). Always a proud Leninist, Gorbachev instituted a New Economic Plan, but the Soviet Union had no entrepreneurs or free market experience from a capitalist past. It only had a large black economy that existed because most of the raw materials and equipment were stolen from the state.

The Soviet sociologist Tatyana Zaslavskaya later summed up the mental state of the Soviet populace:

> The primary reasons for the need for perestroika were not the sluggish economy and the rate of technological development but an underlying mass alienation of working people from significant social goals and values. This social alienation is rooted in the economic system formed in the 1930s, which made state property, run by a vast bureaucratic apparatus, the dominant form of ownership.... For 50 years it was said that this was public property and belonged to everyone, but no way was ever found to make workers feel they were the co-owners and masters of the factories, farms, and enterprises. They felt themselves to be cogs in a gigantic machine.[18]

Next, Gorbachev tried to open up the system at the bottom through *glasnost* (openness). Seeking to weaken the hold of the party elite who ran the country, he encouraged more public discussion of problems, including the corruption of the Communist Party. He freed the famed Jewish political prisoner Natan Sharansky and personally informed the dissident icon Andrei Sakharov that he had been released from his exile in Gorki. To Gorbachev's surprise, the Soviet people did not express their gratitude but demanded more openness. *Glasnost* made it much easier for the citizens of the Soviet satellites and the republics within the USSR to express their nationalism and further weaken communism.

Reagan took advantage of Gorbachev's debilitated position to step up negotiations for an end to the Cold War at summits in Geneva and Reykjavik, Iceland. At the latter meeting, Gorbachev accepted Reagan's "zero option" eliminating all intermediate-range nuclear missiles in Europe and in a spirit of "Can you top this?" proposed a 50 percent cut in Soviet and American strategic weapons. Not to be outdone, Reagan suggested phasing out all intercontinental ballistic missiles within a decade. Gorbachev countered by offering to phase out all ballistic missiles by the year 1996 but made his offer contingent on banning the further development of SDI. Reagan saw SDI as essential to guarantee a safe transition to a non-nuclear world. He refused to give up on SDI and the summit ended with bitter words and stony faces. But the leaders of the two nations discovered they shared an interest in the principle of nuclear abolition. As Gaddis concludes, "The logic was Reagan's, but Gorbachev had come to accept it."[19]

The Reykjavik summit demonstrated that Reagan would not abandon his strategy of peace through strength, and that meant not giving up SDI. Like Truman, Reagan understood that the United States should negotiate from a position of strength—or not at all. He did not accept the idea of parity or the versions of détente put forth by Nixon and Kissinger or Carter.

Reagan kept up the pressure, taking his freedom offensive into the heart of the evil empire. He stood at the Brandenburg Gate in front of the Berlin Wall in June 1987 and directly challenged the Kremlin: "Mr. Gorbachev, tear down this wall!"[20]

Reagan's challenge was part of his strategy to force the Soviet Union to make fundamental changes or become obsolete. "Gorbachev saw the handwriting on the Wall," Reagan wrote in his autobiography, "and opted for change." But it was change that would end Soviet communism.

By introducing such populist concepts as *glasnost* and *perestroika*, Gorbachev made consideration of the people as important as the traditional components of the Soviet state: the Communist Party, the KGB, the Soviet army, and the party elite who ran the country (the *nomenklatura*).

For his reforms to work, Gorbachev had to replace old ways with new ways of thinking, and that required diversity, debate, and freedom, which were all unknown in the Soviet Union. The Soviet leader gambled that he could control the virus of freedom he had let loose with *glasnost*, improve the economy and satisfy the consumer desires of the people through *perestroika*, reassure the military and the KGB he was not jeopardizing their role, persuade the *nomenklatura* to relax its grip on the machinery of the state, secure his own position as general secretary of the Communist Party, and above all keep the Soviet Union socialist.

Gorbachev was probably not familiar with Tocqueville, who wrote, "Experience teaches us that the most critical moment for bad governments is the one which witnesses the first steps toward reform."[21] The Soviet Union in the mid-1980s was a very bad government attempting very radical reform.

Resolved to end the Cold War as quickly as he could, Reagan traveled to Moscow in the spring of 1988 for what one biographer described as his premier presidential performance as freedom's advocate. Beneath a gigantic white bust of Lenin at Moscow State University, the president delivered an eloquent televised address to an audience of awed students on the blessings of democracy, individual freedom, and free enterprise. Near the conclusion of his university talk, Reagan quoted the poet Alexander Pushkin, beloved by all Russians, "It's time, my friend, it's time."[22] It was clear he meant it was time for a free Russia. He received a standing ovation from the transfixed students. While Reagan strolled with Gorbachev in Red Square and was his usual genial self, he emphasized the power imbalance between them by declining to issue a joint statement that spoke of "equality" between the U.S. and the Soviet Union.

GORBACHEV'S GAMBLE

By 1987 it was clear that Gorbachev's economic reforms were not working. A frustrated Gorbachev began talking about "democratization" and, in order to enlist the workers in his campaign, suggested reducing the unique role of the Communist Party. He did not seem to realize that he was writing the obituary of the Soviet Union.

But Gorbachev was set on a course for which he could see no alternative. As part of *glasnost*, he initiated in 1988 several political reforms. Class war, he directed, would no longer be the basis of Soviet foreign policy, a step that would have been violently opposed by Lenin and his ideological successors.

The Communist Party found itself the object of withering open criticism. It was accused of gross culpability in the Ukrainian forced famine of 1932–1933, the Great Terror of 1936–1938, and the Katyn Forest massacre of 1940. Non-governmental organizations like Memorial called up a bloody past the party had attempted to erase. To the consternation of party hard-liners, Gorbachev announced that his reforms could be applied in the satellite states of Eastern and Central Europe, not perceiving that liberalization could have explosive consequences.

The unintended result was the collapse of communism in the Soviet satellites. The fall of the Berlin Wall in November 1989 and the other extraordinary events of that year were preceded by decades of political tyranny and economic backwardness. By January 1989 there was scarcely a ruble's worth of difference between a Third World nation and a member of the Warsaw Pact, the group of Eastern and Central European nations who served at Moscow's pleasure. While the West enjoyed remarkable prosperity and personal freedom, the East had fallen into an economic and political morass. Eastern Europe's industrial sector was a monument to bureaucratic inefficiency and waste and the source of widespread environmental degradation.

The once-impenetrable Iron Curtain was being breached by modern communications and technology, allowing the peoples of Eastern Europe to see how the other half of Europe lived. Increasingly, Poles, Hungarians, Czechs, East Germans, and other nationalities demanded change and reform, not only in the marketplace but in the realm of human rights and civil liberties.

Just as the invasion of Poland in 1939 triggered World War II, the emergence in 1980 of the Polish trade movement Solidarity laid the foundation for the peaceful revolution that brought down communism in Eastern Europe at the end of the decade. For the millions living under it, writes Adam Ulam, communism had come to mean "an overgrown, inefficient, and arrogant bureaucracy, with economic and technological backwardness, and with industrial pollution and devastation of the environment." Although the Polish government outlawed Solidarity and declared a state of martial law, the government and the people both understood that "Marxism-Leninism and the party professing it had been...rejected by the very class whose viewpoint and interest they purported to represent."[23]

THE YEAR OF MIRACLES

In February 1989, Václav Havel was jailed in Prague for participating in human rights protests, but the protests continued. After months of strikes, roundtable talks began in Poland between leaders of the still-outlawed Solidarity union and the communist government. The Polish government had insisted that Solidarity was a "spent force," but as the Polish economy worsened, it was forced to "reckon with ideas they could not squelch and men they could not subdue."[24] In March, seventy-five thousand people demonstrated in Budapest on the anniversary of the 1848 revolution, demanding the withdrawal of Soviet troops and free elections.

In April, Solidarity and the Polish government agreed to the first open elections since World War II. In May, the Hungarian government started to dismantle the Iron Curtain along its border with Austria, allowing East Germans to cross over into West Germany. Thousands did.

In June 1989, the Polish Solidarity movement won an overwhelming victory over their communist opponents in the Soviet bloc's first free elections in forty years. The same month, Imre Nagy, who had led the 1956 Hungarian uprising against Soviet domination, was given a hero's burial in Budapest. Gorbachev reminded the Council of Europe in July that he rejected the Brezhnev Doctrine: "Any interference in domestic affairs and any attempts to restrict the sovereignty of states, both friend and allies or any others, are inadmissible."[25]

In October hundreds of thousands of people began demonstrating every Monday evening in East Germany, leading to the forced resignation of Communist Party boss Erich Honecker, who had boasted in January that the Berlin Wall would stand for another hundred years. On November 9, 1989, a tidal wave of East Germans poured across the West Berlin border when travel restrictions were lifted, and the Berlin Wall came tumbling down.

The year of counterrevolutions ended with the overthrow and execution of the despot Nicolae Ceausescu in Romania and the election of Václav Havel as the president of Czechoslovakia's first non-communist government since the 1948 coup engineered by Moscow.

The waves of liberty, however, did not reach the shores of China. In the spring of 1989, pro-democracy Chinese students, inspired in part by the events in Eastern Europe, were demonstrating by the many thousands in Tiananmen Square in the heart of Beijing. For a short while, it seemed to Western observers as if the leaders of Communist China might follow Gorbachev's example and allow meaningful political as well as economic liberalization. They underestimated the willingness of Deng Xiaoping and other communist leaders to use maximum force to eliminate any threat to their political control. On June 4, 1989, just two weeks after Gorbachev had visited China for a "socialist summit" with Deng, Chinese troops and tanks ruthlessly crushed the protests in Tiananmen Square, killing hundreds and perhaps thousands of defenseless students.

As China's "paramount" leader, Deng had taken the measure of Mao and announced that he was right 70 percent of the time and wrong 30 percent of the time. The Cultural Revolution and the Great Leap Forward were among the mistakes, but among the things Mao had done right were making China once again a great power, maintaining the political monopoly of the Communist Party, and opening relations with the United States as a counterweight to the Soviet Union. The most important of these was the unchallenged political authority of the Party.

Deng's most significant action, beginning in 1979, was to leaven China's command economy with free-market reforms, transforming the country into a global economic power in less than two decades.

PRESIDENT BUSH

George Herbert Walker Bush was the last American president of the Cold War. By instinct and experience, Bush placed stability at the center of his foreign policy. Confronted with fast-moving events, he preferred to move cautiously. He was not a ground-up cold warrior like Truman, a seasoned anticommunist like Reagan, or a theoretical realist like Nixon—he was the quintessential man of the middle. A New Englander by birth and a Texan by choice, Bush received the Distinguished Flying Cross for his combat bravery as a torpedo bomber pilot in the navy during World War II. This background, and his Episcopal faith, made Bush the ultimate public servant in a career that stretched from Congress and the UN to the CIA and a diplomatic post in Beijing.

Bush's time at the United Nations and in China accounted for his passive reaction to the events in Eastern Europe and Tiananmen Square in 1989. "The long-run framework of Bush foreign policy was very deliberate," the president and his national security adviser, Brent Scowcroft, explain in a co-authored memoir of the pivotal years 1989–1991, "encouraging, guiding, and managing change without provoking backlash." They admit they were not prepared for the sudden collapse of communism in Eastern and Central Europe: "Did we see what was coming when we took office? No, we did not, nor could we have planned [for] it." Scowcroft recalls that he shared the doubts of conservative Republicans about Gorbachev's true intentions:

> I was suspicious of Gorbachev's motives and skeptical about his prospects.... I thought Gorbachev remained a communist, committed to a socialist future for the Soviet Union. Through glasnost ("openness") and perestroika ("restructuring") he sought to revitalize the USSR and strengthen its economy.... My fear was that Gorbachev could talk us into disarming without the Soviet Union having to do anything fundamental in its own military structure and that, in a decade or so, we could face a more serious threat than ever before.[26]

The skepticism extended to Gorbachev's remarkable speech at the United Nations in December 1988 in which the Soviet leader renounced the ideological struggle that had occupied the Soviet Union and the West since 1917 and proclaimed a new era in which "the common values of humanity must be the determining priority in international politics." He again repudiated the Brezhnev Doctrine: "Freedom of choice [for a nation] is a universal principle, which knows no exceptions."[27] Bush's national security team—led by Scowcroft, Secretary of State James Baker, and Secretary of Defense Dick Cheney—asked themselves: Did Gorbachev mean it?

Some scholars argue that the Cold War ended in December 1988 with neither a winner nor a loser. They assert that the Soviet Union simply withdrew from the arms race and relinquished control over regimes dependent on economic subsidies for their survival. But such a reading ignores Moscow's serious attempts over the next two years to encourage socialist (i.e., communist) reform in Eastern and Central Europe and to retain control over the several nations of the USSR, including the Baltic states.[28]

Like all new administrations, the Bush administration sought to differentiate itself from the previous one, headed by Ronald Reagan. Thus there is Bush's reference to "a kinder, gentler nation" in his acceptance of the Republican presidential nomination and his go-slow approach to U.S.-Soviet relations.

One of Bush's first acts was to order an administration-wide survey of U.S. foreign policy with an emphasis on the Soviet Union. In Scowcroft's words, the result was a disappointing "big picture" document short on detail and substance. So the president turned to an analysis of Gorbachev's policies and intentions drafted by a group of NSC staffers headed by Condoleezza Rice, a Russian specialist and a future national security adviser and secretary of state under George W. Bush. Since the Soviet Union was in the midst of domestic turmoil and looking to the outside world for help to rebuild its failing system, Rice said, the United States should seek to "transform" the behavior of the Soviet Union at home and abroad.

Although Scowcroft calls the recommendation "a distinct and positive departure for U.S. policy," it was consistent with NSDD 73, approved by Reagan, which had urged the United States to work toward "a fundamental change of the Soviet system." The Rice paper became the "blueprint" for crafting policy toward the Soviet Union in the early Bush administration, albeit with what Scowcroft calls "extensive revision" because of the rapidly unfolding events in Eastern Europe. In a series of speeches in early 1989, Bush outlined a strategy aimed at encouraging a "reformed" Soviet Union capable of playing "a trustworthy role in the community of nations."[29] It was a rational, realistic policy but was soon superseded by the mostly bloodless revolution occurring behind a visibly cracking Iron Curtain. In all, some 110 million people in six countries were affected by the unexpected events in 1989.

Rightly described as a year of miracles, 1989 began with Václav Havel in jail and ended with him as the president of Czechoslovakia. At the start of the year, the Soviet sphere of influence in Eastern and Central Europe seemed secure, but as we have seen, radical change was sweeping across the region. In May a Gorbachev aide wrote privately that "Socialism in Eastern Europe is disappearing." In October, the spokesman for the Soviet foreign ministry was asked what remained of the Brezhnev Doctrine. He responded wryly: "You know the Frank Sinatra song 'My Way'? Hungary and Poland are doing it their way. We now have the Sinatra Doctrine."[30] The collapse of communism from Berlin to Bucharest ended Gorbachev's hope of a reformed but still socialist region led by Moscow. It also ignited a nationalist fervor within the numerous non-Russian peoples of the Soviet Union that had long been suppressed.

One of the most dramatic and yet peaceful acts of rebellion took place on August 23, 1989, the fiftieth anniversary of the 1939 Molotov-Ribbentrop Non-Aggression Pact. Two million persons from Estonia, Latvia, and Lithuania joined hands along the 403-mile road that connected the Baltic capitals to protest the illegal Soviet occupation. One year later, the three republics had virtually declared their independence, although the United States, fearing a Soviet backlash, urged their leaders to "negotiate" with Moscow.

Under Bush and in pursuit of stability, the United States played a minor role in the liberating events of 1989. While proclaiming his dedication to a "whole and free" Europe, the president kept worrying how the Soviets might react to the accelerating collapse of communism in Eastern and Central Europe. He recalls that "we were all haunted by the crushing of the uprisings in Hungary in 1956 and in Prague in 1968. We did not want to provoke a similar disaster." The day the Berlin Wall fell, he held an impromptu press conference in the Oval Office.

Asked "how elated" he felt, the president replied evenly, "I'm very pleased." Bombarded by critics for his seeming lack of enthusiasm, Bush wrote in his diary that "we had to be careful not to upset the process.... A wrong move could destroy the joy we were witnessing." He dismissed summarily the suggestion, made by a prominent Democratic senator, that he go to Berlin to "dance" on the wall.[31]

Ever the realist, Scowcroft acknowledges that the Bush administration's Eastern European policy was not a catalyst in the fall of the wall and the collapse of communism in Eastern Europe. Perhaps unconsciously, he writes, "our policy evolved...from quietly supporting the transformation to cultivating Soviet acquiescence, even collaboration, in them." The disappearance of the Berlin Wall, he said, pushed to center stage the critical question of German reunification and ultimately "the future of Europe."[32]

ONE GERMANY

In late November 1989, without consulting any allies, West German chancellor Helmut Kohl suddenly announced a ten-point program calling for free elections in East Germany and the eventual "reunification" of Germany within a "pan-European framework." President Bush immediately endorsed the plan and pressed Kohl to accept NATO membership for a reunified Germany, arguing that deeper European integration was essential for the West's acceptance of reunification.

When Britain and France as well as the Soviet Union expressed serious reservations about a united Germany, the U.S. State Department suggested a "2 + 4" solution—the two Germanys would negotiate the particulars of reunification while the four occupying powers—Britain, France, the United States, and the USSR—would work out the international details. Bush facilitated Soviet acceptance of the controversial plan (Politburo hard-liners constantly referred to the twenty million Russians who had died at German hands in World War II) with a grain and trade agreement and a commitment to speed up arms control negotiations. In turn, the West German government made substantial economic concessions of many billions of dollars to the Soviets.

In amazingly short order, and due in large part to the skillful diplomacy of the United States, the Treaty on German Unity was signed by representatives of East and West Germany on August 31, 1990, and approved by both legislatures the following month. Final approval was given by the four Allied powers on October 2. Forty-five years after the end of World War II and forty-one years after Germany's division, the German Democratic Republic ceased to exist, and the country was reunited.[33]

After less than a year of negotiations, Bush writes, "we had accomplished the most profound change in European politics and security for many years, without confrontation, without a shot fired, and with all Europe still on the best and most peaceful of terms." "For me," says Scowcroft, "the Cold War ended when the Soviets accepted a united Germany in NATO."[34] But as we shall see, the Cold War was not yet over.

SUMMIT TIME

The first of the three Bush-Gorbachev summit meetings did not take place until December 1989 in Malta, where Bush emphasized the need for "superpower cooperation," choosing to overlook that the Soviet Union was no longer a superpower by any reasonable criterion and that Marxism-Leninism in Eastern Europe was headed for Reagan's "ash-heap of history."

The second summit was in May 1990 in Washington, D.C., where the emphasis was on economics. Gorbachev arrived in a somber mood, conscious that his country's economy was nearing free fall and nationalist pressures were splitting the Soviet Union. Although a virtual pariah at home, the Soviet leader was greeted by large, friendly American crowds. Bush tried to help, granting most-favored-nation trading status to the Soviet Union. Gorbachev appealed to American businessmen to start new enterprises in the USSR, but what could Soviet citizens afford to buy? In Moscow the bread lines stretched around the block. A month later, NATO issued a sweeping statement called the London Declaration, proclaiming that the Cold War was over and that Europe had entered a "new, promising era."[35] But the Soviet Union, although teetering, still stood.

At the third and final Bush-Gorbachev summit, in Moscow in July 1991, the two men signed the first Strategic Arms Reduction Treaty, eliminating a wide range of strategic weapons, building on the Intermediate-Range Nuclear Forces treaty signed by Reagan and Gorbachev four years earlier. The nuclear arms race, the most frightening part of the Cold War, had effectively come to an end. Bush acknowledged Gorbachev's help in the Persian Gulf War earlier that year and spoke of future bilateral cooperation in Africa, Asia, the Middle East, and Central

America. Tellingly he did not include Eastern and Central Europe in his list of regions.

Bush explained his sustained efforts to help Gorbachev in his diary: "My view is, you dance with who is on the dance floor. [Y]ou especially don't... [encourage] destabilization.... I wanted to see stable, and above all peaceful, change. I believed the key to this would be a politically strong Gorbachev and an effectively working central structure."[36] Still in pursuit of stability, he stopped in Kiev on the way home from the Moscow summit to praise Gorbachev for his "astonishing achievements" and to lecture the Ukrainian Parliament:

> Freedom is not the same as independence. Americans will not support those who seek independence in order to replace a far-off tyranny with a local despotism. They will not aid those who promote a suicidal nationalism based upon ethnic hatred.[37]

Ukrainians, who had suffered under Soviet despotism for some eighty years, bristled at Bush's words, which were ridiculed by a *New York Times* columnist as a "chicken Kiev" speech.[38] Scowcroft later argued that the reference to "local despotism" was not directed "specifically" at Ukraine, but critics justifiably charged that the president seemed to be trying to keep the Soviet Union intact.[39]

Just as dismaying to former republics of the USSR seeking independence from Moscow was Bush's tepid reaction in early 1991 to the Soviet crackdown in the Baltic states. Soviet troops and tanks, backed by the "Black Berets" of the Ministry of Defense, seized control of Lithuanian television and press facilities in an unsuccessful attempt to bring down the democratically elected government. Fourteen Lithuanians were killed and several more wounded. A week later, Soviet forces carried out a similar operation in Latvia, killing half a dozen Latvians. Gorbachev denied he had ordered the assaults but did not condemn them, perhaps trying to mollify the hard-liners in the Politburo. Bush publicly called the attacks "disturbing" and privately wrote to Gorbachev that unless there was a "peaceful" resolution of the USSR-Baltic conflict, the United States would withdraw its support of all the economic and trade agreements reached at the recent summit. "I urge you," he wrote, "to take concrete steps to prevent the further use of force and intimidation against the Baltic peoples and their elected leaders."[40] Gorbachev got the message: there were no more Black Beret "incidents."

The shrinking Soviet Union received another major blow when the biggest republic, Russia, elected its own president, Boris Yeltsin. A former Politburo member turned militant anticommunist, Yeltsin announced his intention to abolish the Communist Party, dismantle the Soviet Union, and declare Russia to be "an independent democratic capitalist state."[41]

For the remaining Stalinists in the Politburo, this was the final unacceptable act. Barely three weeks after the Bush-Gorbachev summit in Moscow, the head of the KGB, the Soviet defense and interior ministers, and other hard-liners—the so-called "Gang of Eight"—launched a coup. They placed Gorbachev under house arrest while he was vacationing in the Crimea, proclaiming a state of emergency and themselves the new leaders of the Soviet Union. They called in tanks and troops from outlying areas and ordered them to surround the Russian Parliament, where Yeltsin had his office.

Some eight decades earlier, Lenin had stood on a tank to announce the coming of Soviet communism. Now Yeltsin proclaimed its end by climbing onto a tank outside the Parliament and declaring that the coup was "unconstitutional." He urged all Russians to follow the law of the legitimate government of Russia. Within minutes, the Russian defense minister stated that "not a hand will be raised against the people or the duly elected president of Russia." A Russian officer responded, "We are not going to shoot the president of Russia."[42]

The image of Yeltsin boldly confronting the Gang of Eight was flashed around the world by the Western television networks, especially America's CNN, none of whose telecasts were blocked by the coup plotters. The pictures convinced President Bush (on vacation in Maine) and other Western leaders to condemn the coup and praise Yeltsin and other resistance leaders.

The attempted coup, dubbed the "vodka putsch" because of the inebriated behavior of a coup leader at a televised news conference, collapsed after three short days. When Gorbachev returned to Moscow, he found that Boris Yeltsin was in charge. Most of the organs of power of the Soviet Union had effectively ceased to exist or had been transferred to the Russian government. Gorbachev tried to act as if nothing had changed, announcing, for example, that there was a need to "renew" the Communist Party.[43] He was ignored. The people clearly wanted an end to the party and him. He was the first

Soviet leader to be derided at the annual May Day parade, when protestors atop Lenin's tomb in Red Square displayed banners reading, "Down with Gorbachev! Down with Socialism and the fascist Red Empire. Down with Lenin's party."[44]

A supremely confident Yeltsin banned the Communist Party and transferred all Soviet agencies to the control of the Russian republic. The Soviet republics of Ukraine and Georgia declared their independence. As the historian William H. Chafe writes, the Soviet Union itself had fallen "victim to the same forces of nationalism, democracy, and anti-authoritarianism that had engulfed the rest of the Soviet empire."[45] President Bush at last accepted the inevitable—the unraveling of the Soviet Union. At a cabinet meeting on September 4, he announced that the Soviets and all the republics would and should define their own future "and that we ought to resist the temptation to react to or comment on each development." Clearly, he said, "the momentum [is] toward greater freedom." The last thing the United States should do, he said, is to make some statement or demand that would "galvanize opposition...among the Soviet hard-liners."[46] However, opposition to the new non-communist Russia was thin or scattered; most of the hard-liners were either in jail or exile.

On December 12, Secretary of State James Baker, borrowing liberally from the rhetoric of President Reagan, delivered an address titled "America and the Collapse of the Soviet Empire." "The state that Lenin founded and Stalin built," Baker said, "held within itself the seeds of its demise.... As a consequence of Soviet collapse, we live in a new world. We must take advantage of this new Russian Revolution." While Baker praised Gorbachev for helping to make the transformation possible, he made it clear that the United States believed his time had passed.[47] President Bush quickly sought to make Yeltsin an ally, beginning with the coalition he formed to conduct the Gulf War.

A despondent Gorbachev, not quite sure why it had all happened so quickly, officially resigned as president of the Soviet Union on Christmas Day 1991—seventy-four years after the Bolshevik Revolution. Casting about for reasons, he spoke of a "totalitarian system" that prevented the Soviet Union from becoming "a prosperous and well-to-do country," without acknowledging the role of Lenin, Stalin, and other communist dictators in creating and sustaining that totalitarian system. He referred to "the mad militarization" that had crippled "our economy, public attitudes and morals" but accepted no blame for himself or the generals who had spent up to 40 percent of the Soviet budget on the military. He said that "an end has been put to the cold war" but admitted no role for any Western leader in ending the war.

After just six years, the unelected president of a non-existent country stepped down, still in denial.[48] That night, the hammer and sickle came down from atop the Kremlin, replaced by the blue, white, and red flag of Russia. It is an irony of history, notes Adam Ulam, that "the claim of Communism being a force for peace among nations should finally be laid to rest in its birthplace."[49] Looking back at America's longest war, Martin Malia writes, "The Cold War did not end because the contestants reached an agreement; it ended because the Soviet Union disappeared."[50]

When Gorbachev reached for the pen to sign the document officially terminating the USSR, he discovered it had no ink. He had to borrow a pen from the CNN television crew covering the event. It was a fitting end for someone who was never a leader like Harry Truman or Ronald Reagan, who had clear goals and the strategies to reach them. Gorbachev's attempt to do too much too quickly, the historians Edward Judge and John Langdon conclude, "coupled with his underestimation of the potency of the appeal of nationalism, split the Communist party and wrecked the Soviet Union."[51] Gorbachev experimented, wavered, and at last wearily accepted the dissolution of one of the bloodiest regimes in history. He deserves credit (if not the Nobel Peace Prize) for recognizing that brute force would not save socialism in the Soviet Union or its satellites.[52]

Revisionist historians still call the policy of containment an overreaction. They argue that it led the United States to prop up undemocratic regimes and to make egregious blunders like the Vietnam War. But their number is small and dwindling. Far more prevalent are scholars who have followed the documents like Michael Kort, who writes, "The case for containment as being both necessary and successful appears to be quite solid." The historians John Spanier and Steven W. Hook are more emphatic in their assessment: containment facilitated the "defeat of the second totalitarian challenge to Western-style democracy in the 20th century."[53]

An essential ingredient of containment was the power of ideas. American support for the ideas of democracy, freedom, and human rights had an enormous impact on dissidents behind the Iron Curtain. They listened to broadcasts from the Voice of America, Radio Liberty, and the BBC and took full advantage of the Helsinki Accords. In Martin Walker's words, the accords served as "the West's secret weapon, a time bomb planted in the heart of the Soviet empire."[54] A decisive initiative of Reagan-style containment, according to Paul Johnson, was SDI, which added substantially "to the stresses on the Soviet economy." Vladimir Lukhim, a Soviet foreign policy expert and an ambassador to the United States, said: "It is clear that SDI accelerated our catastrophe by at least five years."[55]

Unlike most protracted conflicts, writes Carole K. Fink, the Cold War ended without a formal surrender or celebration, but its demise affected most of the world. Former clients of Moscow like Cuba, Vietnam, North Korea, and the Palestinians were forced to rely on their own resources. The former Eastern and Central European satellites gravitated toward the West. India and other socialist-leaning Third World countries moved toward a market economy. The United States remained the sole superpower, with all the attendant challenges and responsibilities.[56]

The American president who effectively wrote *finis* to the Cold War was Ronald Reagan, who came into office with a clear set of ideas he had developed over a lifetime of study. He forced the Soviet Union to abandon its goal of world communism by challenging its legitimacy, regaining superiority in the arms race, and using human rights as a powerful psychological weapon. Reagan had the self-confidence and the grace, once the Cold War was over, to commend Gorbachev for admitting that "Communism was not working" and introducing "the beginnings of democracy, individual freedom, and free enterprise" into the Soviet system.[57] But Gorbachev was never able to anticipate the inevitable outcome of the powerful forces he was unleashing. By the time Reagan left office in January 1989, the Reagan Doctrine had achieved its goal—the last leader of the Soviet system had acknowledged "the failures of Marxism-Leninism and the futility of Russian imperialism."[58]

Lech Wałęsa, the founder of the trade union movement that confronted and ultimately brought down communism in Poland and prepared the way for the end of communism throughout Eastern and Central Europe, put his feelings about Reagan simply, "We in Poland...owe him our liberty."[59] So do we who never lived under communism, as well as the tens of millions behind the Iron Curtain who were caught up in one of the longest and

most destructive conflicts in human history—the Cold
War.

CONCLUSION

LESSONS FROM THE COLD WAR

A ll great historical periods and events are instructive. The Cold War is no exception. It offers lasting lessons that can help us deal with the challenges of the present and the future.

What then are the major lessons of the birth and the death of the Cold War that can be applied to the conduct of U.S. foreign policy today? The world has changed since 1945, when the Cold War began, and 1991, when it ended, but certain things remain true.

IDEAS MATTER

Contrary to Machiavelli and his modern-day *Realpolitik* disciples, power is not everything, even in totalitarian regimes. The philosophical ideas undergirding the regime matter as well, because they guide governments and help us to understand their conduct.

The United States has been shaped by ideas drawn from its founding principles. Likewise, the Soviet regime, from beginning to end, was shaped by the principles of Marxism-Leninism. Gorbachev initiated *glasnost* and then *perestroika* in order to save Soviet communism, not to initiate Western democracy. When communists in the Soviet Union and Eastern Europe admitted they no longer believed in communism, they undermined the ideological foundations of their power and authority.

After the Soviet Union collapsed, Gorbachev acknowledged that it had been built on sand, socialist sand. He admitted reluctantly, "The Achilles heel of socialism was the inability to link the socialist goal with the provision of incentives for efficient labor and the encouragement of initiative on the part of individuals. It became clear in practice that a market provides such incentives best of all."[1] Boris Yeltsin was more to the point: "The world can breathe a sigh of relief. The idol of communism, which spread everywhere social strife, animosity, and unparalleled brutality, which instilled fear in humanity, has collapsed."[2]

Similarly, the mullahs who govern Iran—like the radicals behind ISIS—are guided by their commitment to a militant Islam, a commitment that shapes their worldview and influences their conduct on the world stage. In China, the communist government struggles to rationalize the contrary demands of economic liberalization and political control. As China's economy inevitably declines, there will be increased pressure for political liberalization.

FRIENDS AND ALLIES, REAL AND POTENTIAL, MATTER

Early and late in the Cold War, the United States called upon and led a grand alliance against the Soviet Union through diplomatic, economic, and strategic instruments such as the Marshall Plan, NATO, the "police action" in Korea, the deployment of Euromissiles to counter the Soviet SS-20s, the "special relationship" with Great Britain, and the multifaceted Reagan Doctrine. When it acted more unilaterally, as in Vietnam, it was not successful.

In contrast, the Soviet Union was never able to command true allegiance from the members of the Warsaw Pact or the various nationalities and peoples within the Soviet empire. The Soviet Union was not a true nation but a conglomeration of captive peoples and nationalities united by the Kremlin and its Red Army. Marxism-Leninism was an alien doctrine imposed on the peoples of Eastern Europe and the Soviet Union by a totalitarian imperial power. Once Western governments began encouraging the people within the "evil empire" to stand up, they did so with increasing confidence and success. The Hungarian Revolution of 1956 was crushed by Soviet tanks, but in 1980, the communist government of Poland could only "ban" the Solidarity union for fear of alienating the West.

LEADERSHIP MATTERS

The history of the Cold War is the biographies of leaders on both sides of the Iron Curtain. It began with Harry Truman and Joseph Stalin and ended with Ronald Reagan, Margaret Thatcher, Pope John Paul II, Václav Havel, Lech Wałęsa, and even Mikhail Gorbachev, who helped end the Cold War by reluctantly abandoning the Brezhnev Doctrine that had propped up the communist regimes of Eastern Europe for decades. Containment might have continued to be the policy of the United States for years if Reagan had not laid down a new way to wage the Cold War—"We win, and they lose."

A firm commitment to freedom is something the presidents who served at the beginning and the end of the Cold War had in common. As important as Ronald Reagan was to the end of the war, there is much to be learned from the American president who was there at its beginning. Harry Truman's Cold War was a conflict between good and evil, between freedom and tyranny, between liberal democracy and totalitarianism, between capitalism and communism. His strategy was to articulate America's basic principles of freedom and democracy, to assist those who lived under such principles to maintain them, and to help those under totalitarianism to realize them in the future.

The United States enjoyed successes in the Cold War when led by clear-eyed visionaries like Truman and Reagan. American leaders like Richard Nixon and George H. W. Bush, who sought to deal with the communist threat through a so-called "realistic" approach, were less successful. Truman and Reagan crafted principled strategies suited to the circumstances each faced. Truman approved the historic Berlin Airlift, which many experts said was at the same time unrealistic and provocative. Reagan, challenging Gorbachev (over the protests of the State Department) to tear down the Berlin Wall, kept up the political pressure on the Soviet leader while negotiating the INF Treaty. Nixon negotiated with the Soviets and went to China thinking he could get Moscow and Beijing to help end the Vietnam War. He assumed they would be pragmatic rather than remain committed to their end goals, but they wanted their ideological enemy to remain bogged down in that quagmire. Bush kept propping up Gorbachev after the fall of the Berlin Wall despite the convincing evidence that the people throughout the Soviet empire had had enough of communism and wanted a new non-communist beginning.

On the other side, the Soviet Union and its satellites were led by aging tyrants like East German communist boss Erich Honecker, who in early 1989 declared that the Berlin Wall would stand for another hundred years. Gorbachev's three immediate predecessors had believed that the Soviet Union could indefinitely spend an estimated 40 percent of its budget on military weapons. Early Soviet rulers like Lenin and Stalin were ruthlessly totalitarian. As they aged they still believed in their ideological right to rule and that socialism would ultimately triumph.

Khrushchev and Brezhnev never renounced the Leninist goal of a socialist world.

STATECRAFT MATTERS

Victory over a determined adversary requires not only strength and resolve but a strategy suited to the times and the nation-states involved. Containment was an appropriate strategy in the beginning of the Cold War when the United States was sorting out its domestic and foreign responsibilities and the Soviet Union was in place and in power in Eastern Europe. Forty years later, the United States could take the offensive against an economically weakened Soviet Union and its communist satellites, which had failed to deliver the goods to their peoples and whose Marxist ideology was disintegrating.

A successful U.S. foreign policy depends on the exercise of prudence. It is impossible to predetermine the extent, priority, and immediacy of the nation's security requirements—they constantly shifted throughout the Cold War as the balance of world forces changed. Likewise, it is impossible to predetermine the challenges and opportunities for furthering American principles and interests in the world today. It is impossible therefore to know beforehand what specific policy prudence will dictate at any particular time and place. The statesman—that is, the wise president guided by his top advisors—must choose the prudent course at that moment.

Cold War policies such as the Marshall Plan and the Reagan Doctrine were prudent. Our economic aid helped World War II allies to get back on their feet and at the same time created markets for our goods. U.S. military support of the mujahideen in Afghanistan turned that conflict into the Soviet Union's Vietnam and helped end the Cold War. Less prudent policies, like Jimmy Carter's human rights fixation, which resulted in a Marxist Nicaragua and an Islamist Iran, and the Nixon-Kissinger détente, which allowed the Soviets to surpass us in strategic weapons, were failures.

A grand strategy for U.S. foreign policy begins with the thesis that the United States should always clearly express its general principles of freedom, democracy, and the rule of law, be politically, economically, and diplomatically active around the world, and engage militarily when it is necessary to defend its vital interests. Those interests include protecting American territory, sea lanes, and airspace; preventing a major hostile power from controlling Europe, East Asia, or the Persian Gulf; ensuring U.S. access to world resources; defending free trade throughout the world; and protecting Americans against threats to their lives and well-being.

Whether it is clashes with Islamic terrorists or long-term challenges from autocratic Russia or Communist China's economic and military attempts to expand its sphere of influence, a prudent foreign policy guided by our founding principles and backed up by our capabilities offers the best path for the United States. That is a strategy for today and tomorrow and for the ages.

COLD WAR TIMELINE

1917

OCTOBER

Led by Vladimir Lenin, the Communist Revolution in Russia puts the Bolsheviks in power.

1922

NOVEMBER

The Russian Civil War ends with the establishment of the Union of Soviet Socialist Republics; Joseph Stalin is appointed general secretary of the Communist Party.

1924

JANUARY 21

Lenin dies after a long illness. Stalin consolidates all political power, ruling the Soviet Union with an iron hand until his death in 1953.

1939

AUGUST 23

The Molotov-Ribbentrop Pact, also known as the Nazi-Soviet Pact, splits Poland and the rest of Eastern Europe between the USSR and Nazi Germany.

1945

FEBRUARY 4–12

Yalta Conference. Roosevelt, Churchill, and Stalin, meeting in the Crimea, agree on free and open elections in Eastern Europe and divide Germany into four occupation zones.

APRIL 12

Franklin D. Roosevelt dies; Harry S. Truman becomes president.

APRIL 25

United Nations founded.

MAY 8

V-E Day. Allies celebrate victory in Europe after the unconditional surrender of Nazi Germany.

JULY 17–AUGUST 2

Potsdam Conference. Meeting in Potsdam, Germany, Truman confirms Stalin's plans to enter the war against Japan. Atlee replaces Churchill as prime minister of Great Britain. U.S. and Britain object to Soviet policies toward Poland and the Black Sea.

AUGUST 14

V-J Day. Allies celebrate Japan's unconditional surrender. World War II ends with Soviets retaining most of the territories they held in 1939 and areas occupied during the war, including parts of Austria, Germany, and Korea. Communists formally control governments in Albania, Bulgaria, and Romania.

DECEMBER
Soviets install communist government in northern Iran.

1946

FEBRUARY 9
Stalin announces that conflicts between the West and USSR are inevitable, charges that capitalism caused World War II, and calls for an industrial build-up in Russia.

FEBRUARY 22
George Kennan sends the Long Telegram from Moscow to Washington, describing inherent Soviet hostility toward Western capitalist societies, especially the United States.

MARCH 5
Churchill delivers his Iron Curtain speech in Fulton, Missouri, proposing an Anglo-American alliance against international communism.

MARCH–MAY
After months of diplomatic protests by the United States, Great Britain, and the United Nations, the Soviets withdraw from Iran. Truman orders preparation of task force to send to the eastern Mediterranean.

AUGUST–OCTOBER
The USSR pressures Turkey to agree to joint control of the Turkish Straits, beginning naval maneuvers in the Black Sea and dispatching troops to the Balkans. In response to a plea from the Turkish government, Truman orders a naval task force to the area and affirms U.S. support of Turkey.

SEPTEMBER
Attempted communist takeover intensifies civil war in Greece.

DECEMBER 19
Indochina War begins.

1947

JANUARY 19
Communists take power in rigged Polish elections in violation of Yalta agreements.

FEBRUARY 21
The British officially inform the United States they can no longer guarantee the security of Greece and Turkey.

MARCH 12
Truman Doctrine. Announcing aid to Greece and Turkey, Truman proposes a policy of supporting free people against anti-democratic forces from within or outside national borders.

JUNE 5
Marshall Plan: With Truman's full backing, Secretary of State George Marshall announces a multi-billion-dollar European Recovery Program of economic aid.

JULY
"Sources of Soviet Conduct" by "X" (George Kennan) published in *Foreign Affairs*, advocating policy of containment of the Soviet Union.

JULY 26
National Security Act signed into law, reorganizing the U.S. military under the Department of Defense and establishing the Joint Chiefs of Staff, the National Security Council, and the CIA.

1948

FEBRUARY 25
Communist coup in Czechoslovakia. Soon after, Congress passes the European Recovery Program (the Marshall Plan).

JUNE 24
Berlin blockade begins.

JULY–SEPTEMBER
UN-supervised free elections lead to the formation of the Republic of Korea in the south; Soviet Union declares the Democratic People's Republic of Korea in the north to be the legitimate government of all Korea.

AUGUST 3
Whittaker Chambers accuses Alger Hiss of espionage at open congressional hearing.

AUGUST–DECEMBER
Communists formally take over Hungary, arresting and executing opponents and controlling the secret police; Cardinal Joseph Mindszenty, primate of Hungary, is imprisoned on December 26.

1949

JANUARY 20
Harry S. Truman is sworn in again as president.

APRIL 4
Formation of the North Atlantic Treaty Organization (NATO), a twelve-nation military alliance intended to protect Western alliance members and contain Soviet expansion.

MAY 12
Berlin blockade ends.

MAY–OCTOBER
The Federal Republic of Germany is established in West Germany; the Soviets declare their zone of East Germany to be the German Democratic Republic.

AUGUST 29
Soviet Union tests an atomic bomb.

OCTOBER 1
Mao Zedong declares the birth of the People's Republic of China after a long civil war between the communists and Chiang Kai-shek's Nationalists; Chiang and other anticommunist Chinese move to the island of Formosa (Taiwan) and set up the government of the Republic of China.

1950

JANUARY
Truman approves development of the hydrogen bomb.

FEBRUARY 9
Senator Joseph McCarthy claims that communists have infiltrated the U.S. State Department.

FEBRUARY 16
The USSR and the People's Republic of China sign a pact of mutual defense.

JUNE 25
Communist North Korea invades South Korea with military support from the Soviet Union.

JUNE 27
Truman and the United Nations call for a defense of South Korea. United States sends forces (eventually joined by forces from sixteen other countries) led by General MacArthur to Korea.

SEPTEMBER 30
Truman approves NSC 68, the outline of a broad defense and foreign policy strategy to counter and challenge the Soviet Union.

1951

MARCH 29

Julius and Ethel Rosenberg are convicted of espionage for their role in giving atomic secrets to the USSR during and after World War II.

JULY 10

Armistice talks begin in Korea.

1952

FEBRUARY

Greece and Turkey join NATO.

JUNE

The European Recovery Program ends, with European industrial output substantially higher than in 1948.

1953

JANUARY 20

Dwight D. Eisenhower is sworn in as president.

MARCH 5

Stalin dies.

JUNE 17

Anticommunist riots in East Berlin suppressed by Soviet and East German forces.

JULY 27

Armistice ends the fighting in Korea, but no peace treaty is signed.

SEPTEMBER 7

Nikita Khrushchev becomes head of the Soviet Communist Party; his main rival is executed in December.

1954

MAY 7

Dien Bien Phu falls to communist Vietminh in Vietnam.

AUGUST

The first Taiwan Straits crisis occurs when the Communist Chinese shell Taiwanese islands; the United States backs the ROC.

SEPTEMBER 8

The Southeast Asian Treaty Organization (SEATO) is founded to resist communist aggression. Member states are Australia, France, New Zealand, Pakistan, Thailand, the Philippines, the United Kingdom, and the United States.

DECEMBER 2

U.S. Senate censures Senator Joseph McCarthy.

1955

FEBRUARY 24

The Baghdad Pact is formed to resist communist aggression in the Middle East, with member states Iran, Iraq, Pakistan, Turkey, and the United Kingdom. The United States becomes an associate member in 1959, when the pact is renamed CENTO after Iraq's withdrawal.

MAY

West Germany joins NATO.

MAY 14

Warsaw Pact established by the USSR and satellites Albania, Poland, Romania, Hungary, East Germany, Czechoslovakia, and Bulgaria.

1956

FEBRUARY 25

Nikita Khrushchev delivers his "secret" de-Stalinization speech at the Twentieth Communist Party Congress.

JUNE 29

Anticommunist protests in Poznan, Poland, are crushed by communist Polish and Soviet forces.

JULY

First American U-2 reconnaissance flights over the Soviet Union.

JULY–NOVEMBER

During the Suez Canal Crisis, Eisenhower pressures Britain and France to accept a UN ceasefire in order to prevent the USSR from assisting Gamal Nasser's Egypt and expanding Soviet presence in the Middle East.

OCTOBER 23

Hungarian Revolution begins, but after two weeks of freedom, students and workers protesting Soviet occupation are violently put down and communist rule is reestablished.

DECEMBER

Communist insurgency sponsored by North Vietnam begins in South Vietnam.

DECEMBER 2

Fidel Castro arrives in Cuba, where he will lead a revolution and establish a communist state.

1957

JANUARY 5

Eisenhower Doctrine—a commitment to defend the Middle East from communist aggression—is announced.

OCTOBER 4

Spuknik I satellite launched by the Soviet Union.

NOVEMBER

Khrushchev publicly claims Soviet missile superiority over the United States, but U-2 flights secretly confirm U.S. superiority.

1958

JANUARY 1

The Common Market established by Western European nations.

MAY

Mao begins the Great Leap Forward, a collectivization of Chinese agriculture that will cause the deaths of tens of millions.

AUGUST

The second Taiwan Straits crisis begins with communist Chinese bombing of Quemoy.

NOVEMBER

The second Berlin crisis begins, with Khrushchev demanding that the West leave Berlin.

1959

JANUARY 1

Fidel Castro takes control of Cuba.

JULY 24

The "Kitchen Debate," an exchange between Khrushchev and Vice President Richard Nixon about the relative levels of abundance produced by capitalism and socialism, takes place at an American cultural exhibition in Moscow. The exchange is captured on videotape and broadcast in the United States and the USSR.

SEPTEMBER

Khrushchev is the first Soviet premier to visit the United States.

1960

MAY 5

Khrushchev announces that the USSR has shot down an American U-2 plane and captured its pilot. United States suspends U-2 flights.

JUNE

The Sino-Soviet split begins.

AUGUST

Communist revolt in Laos begins.

OCTOBER

Khrushchev vehemently protests against American and Western policies at the United Nations, publicly embraces Fidel Castro.

1961

JANUARY 3

Diplomatic relations between the United States and Cuba end.

JANUARY 20

John F. Kennedy is sworn in as president.

APRIL 17

Bay of Pigs invasion. Cuban exiles organized by the CIA land in Cuba, seeking to spark an uprising against Castro's regime. President Kennedy withholds vital air and naval support, and the mission fails.

MAY

First U.S. military advisors are sent to Vietnam.

AUGUST 13

Berlin border is closed by East Germany, followed by construction of the Berlin Wall dividing East and West Berlin. The wall cuts off the flow of thousands of East Germans seeking to migrate to the West.

OCTOBER 31

USSR detonates the most powerful thermonuclear weapon ever tested, with an explosive yield of some fifty megatons.

1962

SEPTEMBER–NOVEMBER

Communist Chinese forces attack India and make claims on numerous areas along the Himalayan border.

OCTOBER

Cuban Missile Crisis erupts when the United States discovers Soviet nuclear missiles in Cuba capable of striking U.S. targets. Kennedy imposes a quarantine and demands the missiles' removal. The Soviets acquiesce, acknowledging the superior military strength of the United States, while the United States agrees to remove its nuclear missiles from Turkey.

NOVEMBER

Publication of Aleksandr Solzhenitsyn's *One Day in the Life of Ivan Denisovich*, based on the author's experiences as a prisoner in the Gulag.

1963

JUNE 20

Hotline enabling direct communication between the White House and the Kremlin is opened.

JUNE 26

Kennedy delivers his "Ich bin ein Berliner" speech in Berlin.

JULY 25

Nuclear test ban treaty between United States, Soviet Union, and Great Britain is signed.

NOVEMBER 1

Ngo Dinh Diem, president of Vietnam, is overthrown and assassinated.

NOVEMBER 22

President John F. Kennedy is assassinated by Marxist Lee Harvey Oswald; Lyndon Johnson is sworn in as president.

1964

AUGUST 7

Senate passes the Gulf of Tonkin Resolution, authorizing U.S. military action in Vietnam.

OCTOBER 14

Khrushchev is replaced by Leonid Brezhnev as general secretary of the Communist Party of the Soviet Union.

OCTOBER 16

Communist China tests its first atomic bomb.

NOVEMBER 3

Lyndon B. Johnson is elected president.

1965

MARCH 2

Extensive U.S. bombing (Operation Rolling Thunder) begins in Vietnam.

MARCH 8–9

First U.S. combat troops arrive in Vietnam.

1966

AUGUST

The Cultural Revolution begins in the PRC.

1967

OCTOBER 21

Thousands of demonstrators picket the Pentagon in protest against U.S. involvement in Vietnam.

1968

JANUARY

North Korea captures USS *Pueblo*; captain and crew are released in December.

JANUARY 5

"Prague Spring" begins in Czechoslovakia.

JANUARY 30

Tet Offensive begins in South Vietnam.

AUGUST 20–21

Warsaw Pact and Soviet troops suppress the "Prague Spring."

1969

JANUARY 20
Richard Nixon is sworn in as president.

MARCH 2
Clash between troops of Soviet Union and People's Republic of China along their joint border.

JUNE 8
President Nixon begins "Vietnamization" of the war in Indochina and announces gradual withdrawal of U.S. troops from Vietnam.

JULY 25
Nixon Doctrine: A pledge to honor treaties, provide a nuclear shield to allies, and provide arms and economic aid to other nations but not U.S. troops.

1970

MARCH 5
Nuclear Non-Proliferation Treaty is ratified.

APRIL 30
Nixon announces invasion of Cambodia. Four students killed in protests at Kent State University.

AUGUST 12
Nonaggression pact between West Germany and the Soviet Union signed.

1971

APRIL
United States ends trade embargo on the People's Republic of China.

AUGUST

India and the USSR sign a twenty-year friendship pact.

1972

FEBRUARY

Nixon becomes the first U.S. president to visit the People's Republic of China.

MAY 26

First Strategic Arms Limitation Treaty (SALT I) and Anti-Ballistic Missile Treaty (ABM Treaty) signed by United States and USSR.

JUNE 17

Break-in at the Democratic National Committee headquarters in Washington, beginning the Watergate scandal.

1973

JANUARY 27

Vietnam Peace Agreement signed in Paris.

MAY 17

Congressional Watergate hearings begin.

1974

FEBRUARY 12

After publication of *The Gulag Archipelago* in the West, Solzhenitsyn is arrested and exiled from the USSR.

AUGUST 9

Richard Nixon resigns the presidency in the face of certain impeachment and conviction and is succeeded by Gerald R. Ford.

SEPTEMBER 12

Communists take power in Ethiopia.

1975

APRIL 17

Cambodia falls to communist Khmer Rouge, who over the next two years engineer the death of one-fifth of the Cambodian population.

APRIL 30

Saigon falls to the North Vietnamese after U.S. Congress refuses further aid, ending the Vietnam War in a communist victory.

MAY 12–15

Khmer Rouge seizes the American merchant ship *Mayaguez* in disputed waters off Cambodia. The ship is recaptured with heavy U.S. casualties in the last official engagement of the Vietnam War.

JUNE–NOVEMBER

Communists take power in Angola and Mozambique.

JULY 30–AUGUST 1

Western powers and USSR sign the Helsinki Accords. The West accepts Soviet borders and increased trade, while Soviets promise to recognize certain human rights.

NOVEMBER 29

Communists take power in Laos.

1976

SEPTEMBER 9

Mao Zedong dies; Cultural Revolution ends.

1977

JANUARY 1

Charter 77 is signed by Czechoslovakian dissidents, including Václav Havel.

JANUARY 20

Jimmy Carter is sworn in as president.

JULY

After years of protesting Soviet repression, especially of Jews, Natan Sharansky is found guilty at a show trial. He will spend years in prisons in Moscow and the Perm Gulag in Siberia.

Soviets continue arms buildup in Eastern Europe, including deployment of SS-20 missiles that can reach targets in Western Europe.

1978

OCTOBER 16

Karol Wojtyła, archbishop of Krakow, Poland, elected pope, taking the name John Paul II.

DECEMBER 25

Communists seize power in Afghanistan.

1979

JANUARY 1

United States and People's Republic of China establish diplomatic relations. U.S. ends official diplomatic relations with longtime ally the Republic of China on Taiwan.

MAY 4

Margaret Thatcher becomes prime minister of Great Britain.

JUNE 2–11

Pope John Paul II visits Poland.

JUNE 18

Carter and Brezhnev sign the SALT II agreement.

JULY 17

Communist Sandinistas, supported by Cuba, topple the Nicaraguan government.

NOVEMBER 4

Iranian militants attack U.S. embassy in Teheran and seize fifty-two hostages, beginning the 444-day Iran hostage crisis.

DECEMBER 12

NATO announces dual-track decision to deploy long-range theater nuclear forces in Western Europe and offers to negotiate with the Soviets on nuclear weapons in Europe.

DECEMBER 27

The Soviet Union responds to a coup in Afghanistan by invading and establishing a pro-Soviet government, becoming entangled in a decade-long civil war.

1980

JANUARY 22

Russian dissident and Nobel laureate Andrei Sakharov protests the Soviet invasion of Afghanistan and is exiled to Gorki, a city closed to foreigners.

JANUARY 24

Carter Doctrine: the United States will respond with force if any country attempts to control the Persian Gulf and threaten U.S. interests there.

AUGUST 31

Communist Polish government legalizes the Solidarity trade union.

NOVEMBER 3

After campaigning on a pledge to restore U.S. military superiority, Ronald Reagan is elected president.

1981

JANUARY 20
Reagan sworn in as president; Iran hostage crisis ends.

APRIL 1
United States suspends aid to Nicaragua.

DECEMBER 13
Polish government arrests Solidarity leaders and declares martial law.

1982

MAY 30
Spain joins NATO.

JUNE 8
Addressing the British Parliament, Reagan predicts that communism is headed for "ash-heap of history."

NOVEMBER 10
Leonid Brezhnev dies and is succeeded by Yuri Andropov as head of USSR.

1983

MARCH 23
Reagan announces the Strategic Defense Initiative (SDI).

SEPTEMBER 1
Soviets shoot down civilian Korean Air Lines Flight 007, flying from Anchorage to Seoul, purportedly in Soviet airspace, killing all 269 aboard, including a member of Congress.

OCTOBER 25
U.S. forces overthrow the Marxist regime in Grenada and restore democracy.

NOVEMBER 23
Deployment of U.S. cruise and Pershing II missiles in Western Europe begins.

1985

FEBRUARY 6
Reagan Doctrine: the United States will support anticommunist fighters in Afghanistan, Nicaragua, Angola, and Cambodia.

MARCH 11
After the deaths of Yuri Andropov and Konstantin Chernenko, Mikhail Gorbachev becomes general secretary of the Communist Party and leader of the Soviet Union.

NOVEMBER
Reagan and Gorbachev meet for the first time at a summit in Geneva and agree to hold more summits.

1986

OCTOBER
Reagan and Gorbachev agree at Reykjavik to remove all intermediate nuclear missiles from Europe; after offering to share nuclear technology, Reagan refuses to give up SDI, which leads to end of the summit.

NOVEMBER
The Iran-Contra scandal breaks.

1987

JUNE 12
Speaking in Berlin before the Brandenburg Gate Reagan challenges Gorbachev to "tear down this wall!"

DECEMBER 8–10
Gorbachev and Reagan sign the INF Treaty, eliminating an entire class of nuclear weapons for the first time.

1988

FEBRUARY 8
Soviet Union announces its withdrawal from Afghanistan.

MAY 31
Speaking at Moscow State University, Reagan says that "it's time" for a new world of friendship, peace, and freedom.

DECEMBER
Gorbachev renounces the Brezhnev Doctrine, saying the USSR will no longer interfere militarily in Eastern Europe.

1989

JANUARY–FEBRUARY
Soviet troops withdraw from Afghanistan.

JANUARY 15
Czech police put down demonstrators, arrest Václav Havel.

JANUARY 20
George H. W. Bush is sworn in as president.

FEBRUARY 14
Sandinista government agrees to free elections in Nicaragua.

MARCH 26
In the first partially free elections in the Soviet Union, non-Communists are elected to the Congress of People's Deputies.

MAY 2
Hungary begins to remove the fence separating it from Austria.

JUNE 3–4

Tiananmen Square Massacre. After weeks of pro-democracy demonstrations, Chinese troops and tanks forcibly end demonstrations, killing hundreds and perhaps thousands of students.

JUNE 4 AND 18

In free Polish elections, Solidarity defeats the communists.

JUNE 16

Imre Nagy, the leader of the 1956 Hungarian Revolution, is given a hero's burial in Budapest.

OCTOBER 9

Massive popular protests begin in Leipzig, East Germany.

NOVEMBER 9

Berlin Wall falls: travel restrictions are lifted, and many thousands of East Germans flood into West Germany.

DECEMBER 25

Romanian dictator Nicolae Ceausescu is overthrown and executed.

DECEMBER 29

Václav Havel becomes president of Czechoslovakia, leading its first non-communist government since 1948.

1990

MARCH 11

Lithuania declares independence from the Soviet Union. Estonia and Latvia soon follow.

MARCH 13

Communist Party loses its monopoly of power in the Soviet Union.

OCTOBER 3

Unification of Germany.

NOVEMBER 18–21

Conventional Armed Forces in Europe Treaty and the Charter of Paris for a New Europe are signed, bringing the Cold War closer to an end; the USSR, however, continues to exist.

1991

JULY 1

Warsaw Pact disbands.

AUGUST 19–21

Hard-liners in the Politburo attempt a coup, placing Gorbachev under house arrest. Boris Yeltsin rallies the people against the Gang of Eight and the coup collapses.

DECEMBER 25

Gorbachev resigns as president of Soviet Union after Russian president Yeltsin bans the Communist Party and assumes all the powers of the old regime. The USSR dissolves, and the Cold War officially ends.

DECEMBER 31

Soviet Union is replaced by fifteen independent states led by Russia.

FOR FURTHER READING AND VIEWING

For readers who would like to learn more about the longest global conflict of the twentieth century, here is a list of recommended histories, memoirs, novels, and feature films and documentaries, as well as selected websites for presidential libraries, government documents, and university centers.

BOOKS

Against All Hope: A Memoir of Life in Castro's Gulag, Armando Valladares (2001). Arrested for his opposition to communism, Valladares spent twenty-two years in Cuban prisons, often in solitary confinement, before finally being released in 1982. His memoir has been compared to *Darkness at Noon* and other classic prison narratives.

An American Life, Ronald Reagan (1990). This official autobiography of our fortieth president is useful for its detailed account of his campaign to defeat communism and eliminate the threat of nuclear weapons—which he regarded as inclusive goals.

The Black Book of Communism: Crimes, Terror, Repression, Stephane Courtois, Nicolas Weth, Jean-Louis Panne, Andrzej Paczkowski, Karel Bartosek, and Jean-Louis Margolin, trans. Jonathan Murphy and Mark Kramer (1999). This international bestseller is indispensable for its careful research and comprehensive examination of the manifold victims and crimes of communism in the twentieth century.

A Century of Violence in Soviet Russia, Alexander N. Yakovlev (2002). A former ambassador and top adviser to Soviet leader Mikhail Gorbachev, Yakovlev draws upon Soviet and Communist Party archives to estimate that 60 million citizens were killed during the Soviet years and millions more died of starvation.

The Cold War: A New History, John Lewis Gaddis (2005). The dean of Cold War historians—a one-time post-revisionist—concludes that the Soviet Union and not the United States was primarily responsible for starting and sustaining the Cold War.

The Collapse of Communism, ed. Lee Edwards (2000). Leading authorities on communism (including Zbigniew Brzezinski, Martin Malia, and Michael Novak) argue that a wide range of forces—political, economic, strategic, and religious—as well as the leadership of principled statesmen and brave dissidents brought about the end of communism in Eastern and Central Europe.

The Columbia Guide to the Cold War, Michael Kort (1998). This excellent introduction to the vast body of information about the Cold War includes a narrative essay, an A to Z encyclopedia of people, places, and things, a concise chronology, and a guide to Cold War resources.

Communism: A History, Richard Pipes (2001). Only a superlative historian like Pipes could describe in just 150 pages the essential ideas of Marxism-Leninism and explain why it collapsed. The main reason: it was "a pseudo-science converted into a pseudo-religion and embodied in an inflexible political regime."

Darkness at Noon, Arthur Koestler (1940). This masterful psychological novel depicts the trial of a veteran Bolshevik who confesses to crimes he did not commit. The "darkness," Koestler shows, flows inevitably from the paranoia of a tyrant like Stalin and the absolute power of an ideology like Marxism-Leninism.

The Double Image, Helen MacInnes (1966). In this story of international espionage, an innocent young American in Paris is caught up with the CIA, MI5, and the French secret service in a hunt that spreads to Greece for an ex-Nazi who turns out to be a Soviet communist. The author of over twenty World War II and Cold War novels, MacInnes is here at the top of her spy story game.

The Fifty Year War: Conflict and Strategy in the Cold War, Norman Friedman (2000). A recognized authority on twentieth century warfare and defense strategy, Friedman integrates geopolitics with the technical and military developments of the last fifty years in this history of what he calls World War III.

The First Cold Warrior: Harry Truman, Containment, and the Remaking of Liberal Internationalism, Elizabeth Edwards Spalding (2006). In a significant reassessment of our thirty-third president, Spalding argues that Truman himself defined and articulated the theoretical underpinnings of containment. Truman, she says, provides a feasible model for the crises facing America in our present age of ideological conflict.

The Fourth Protocol, Frederick Forsyth (1985). Behind the Iron Curtain, an insidious plot against the West is being hatched by the general secretary of the Soviet Union and master spy Kim

Philby. Only a British agent can stop the conspiracy. Set against the backdrop of the nuclear freeze movement, this is a classic thriller by a master of the genre.

The God That Failed, Andre Gide, Richard Wright, Ignazio Silone, Stephen Spender, Arthur Koestler, and Louis Fischer (1950). Six of the world's most famous writers explain why they became Communists and then rejected Communism.

The Great Terror: A Reassessment, Robert Conquest (2008). This is the definitive work about one of the great crimes of the twentieth century—Stalin's bloody purge of the Soviet communist party and his enemies in the 1930s.

Gulag: A History, Anne Applebaum (2003). Applebaum rightly won a Pulitzer Prize for this scrupulously documented history of the Soviet camp system from its origins in the Bolshevik Revolution of 1917 to its collapse in the era of *glasnost*.

The Gulag Archipelago: An Experiment in Literary Investigation, Alexander Solzhenitsyn (1973). This mammoth 1,800-page work is part history, part memoir, part spiritual essay about the role of "redemptive suffering" and the requirement to oppose every form of tyranny over the mind and soul of man. It was Solzhenitsyn who named the forced labor camps "Gulag" and changed the political dialogue of the twentieth century.

Life and Death in Shanghai, Nien Cheng (1987). This widely acclaimed memoir recounts the harsh persecution and years of imprisonment that Cheng suffered during Mao Zedong's Cultural Revolution—and her courageous refusal to confess a lie.

Memoirs: 1925–1950, George F. Kennan (1967). A veteran diplomat and superb writer, Kennan is usually credited with being the author of the U.S. policy of containment. A small but growing group of scholars believe that more credit should go to the man from Missouri—Harry Truman.

Memoirs: Year of Decisions (1955), *Memoirs: Years of Trial and Hope* (1956), Harry S. Truman. Initially dismissed as out of his depth as our chief executive, President Truman generated the U.S. foreign policy that contained communism in Europe and prevented the communist takeover of South Korea, among other Cold War accomplishments.

Modern Times: The World from the Twenties to the Eighties, Paul Johnson (1983). This superbly written sweeping narrative of the world pays particular attention to the deadly "social engineering" of communist regimes.

1984, George Orwell (1948). Warning against a ubiquitous, omnipotent government that molds the past and therefore the present, this iconic novel is a passionate defense of individual freedom.

One Day in the Life of Ivan Denisovich, Alexander Solzhenitsyn (1962). This Nobel Prize–winning novella first exposed the brutal reality of the vast network of Soviet concentration camps.

Perestroika: New Thinking for Our Country and the World, Mikhail Gorbachev (1987). The general secretary of the Soviet communist party offers a blueprint for "new" thinking which takes its inspiration from the old Leninist thinking. As he writes, "we are looking within socialism, rather than outside it, for the answers to all questions."

Present at the Creation: My Years at the State Department, Dean Acheson (1969). Generally regarded as a hard-liner, Acheson served as secretary of state to President Truman and as a trusted adviser to Presidents John F. Kennedy and Lyndon B. Johnson.

Reagan in His Own Hand, edited by Kiron K. Skinner, Annelise Anderson, and Martin Anderson (2001). A collection of Ronald Reagan's pre-presidential writing on a far-reaching range of subjects that details his pro-freedom vision for America at home and abroad.

The Rise and Fall of the Soviet Empire, Brian Crozier (1999). An eminent British writer and historian recounts the birth, life, and sudden death of the Soviet empire. The book provides a trove of original documents from the Kremlin and other communist archives.

The Story of Henri Tod, William F. Buckley Jr. (1984). In the summer of 1961, CIA operative Blackford Oakes is delegated by President John F. Kennedy to prevent Henri Tod, who heads a Germany-wide anti-communist underground, from stopping the building of the Berlin Wall. This is a first-rate spy thriller filled with Buckley's spot-on portraits of Cold War leaders like JFK.

Three Who Made a Revolution: A Biographical History, Bertram D. Wolfe (1948). The author presents the interlocking life stories of the three revolutionaries who led the Bolshevik Revolution and altered world history—Vladimir Lenin, Leon Trotsky, and Joseph Stalin. A classic work of research and analysis.

Witness, Whittaker Chambers (1952). Chambers tells the story of his youthful disillusion with the West, participation in espionage at the highest levels of the U.S. government, and final break with communism in this bestselling autobiography. William F. Buckley Jr. called Chambers "the most important American defector from communism."

A World Transformed, George Bush and Brent Scowcroft (1998, 2011). The president and his national security advisor provide a "you are there" account of their conduct of U.S. foreign policy at the end of the Cold War, including the response to Iraq's Saddam Hussein and Communist China's Tiananmen Square.

FILMS

Bridge of Spies (2015). 141 minutes. Director: Steven Spielberg. Stars: Tom Hanks, Mark Rylance. A true cold war story based on the swap of Soviet master spy Rudolf Abel for the captured American

U-2 pilot Francis Gary Powers. This is not a cynical LeCarre tale in which both sides are morally equivalent, but a taut Spielberg drama in which U.S. lawyer James Donovan (played by Hanks) outwits the communists, obtaining the release not only of Powers but an American student wrongfully imprisoned.

Charlie Wilson's War (2007). 102 minutes. Director: Mike Nichols. Stars: Tom Hanks, Julia Roberts. A biographical drama that recounts the true story of U.S. Rep. Charlie Wilson (D-Texas), who partnered with the CIA to launch Operation Cyclone that successfully (and secretly) supported the Afghan mujahideen in their battle against the Soviet occupation of Afghanistan.

From Russia with Love (1963). 118 minutes. Director: Terence Young. Stars: Sean Connery, Robert Shaw, Lotte Lenya. James Bond (Connery) takes on terrorists, communists, and beautiful women in this early Bond movie and prevails over all of them. When President Kennedy said that *From Russia with Love* was one of his favorite novels, it became an international bestseller. He would have also praised the film version.

The Green Berets (1968). 141 minutes. Directors: John Wayne and Ray Kellogg. Stars: John Wayne, David Janssen. This unabashedly patriotic film portrays the dangerous mission of an elite Special Forces unit in Vietnam.

The Hunt for Red October (1990). 135 minutes. Director: John McTiernan. Stars: Sean Connery, Alec Baldwin. Based on the Tom Clancy novel that became a bestseller in part due to President Reagan's enthusiastic recommendation, the movie tracks Soviet submarine captain Marko Ramius (Connery) as he ignores Moscow's orders and heads for the East Coast of the United States. Equipped with stealth technology, his nuclear-armed sub is virtually invisible. CIA agent Jack Ryan (Baldwin) boards an American sub to determine Raimus's intentions in this taut technical thriller.

The Inner Circle (1991). 137 minutes. Director: Andrei Koncha-
lovsky. Stars: Tom Hulce, Alexandre Zbruev (as Stalin). A film
projectionist and loyal party member shows Western cowboy
movies to Stalin and his often drunken comrades in the 1930s
while overlooking the cruel oppression of the Soviet dictator. The
film focuses on the fate of a single Jewish intellectual rather than
the millions dying in the Gulag. Filmed in the Kremlin.

The Lives of Others (2006). 137 minutes. Director: Florian Henckel
von Donnersmarck. Stars: Ulrich Muhe, Sebastian Koch, Martina
Gedeck. German with English subtitles. Winner of the 2007
Academy Award for the best foreign-language film of the year.
Muhe portrays a veteran *stasi* (secret police) officer in East Germany in the mid-1980s who is ordered to surveil a suspect play-
wright and his actress-lover. Gradually, the communist agent is
drawn into their lives and eventually decides to cover up their
"subversive" activities. A powerful film about the age-old struggle
of man versus the state.

Red Corner (1997). 122 minutes. Director: Jon Avnet. Stars: Richard
Gere, Bai Ling. Gere is an American businessman in Communist
China who is falsely accused of a capital crime. Defense lawyer
Ling wins Gere his freedom by uncovering a high-ranking con-
spiracy and corruption in the Chinese government. Unsurpris-
ingly, the film is banned in the People's Republic of China.

Red Dawn (1984). 114 minutes. Director: John Milius. Stars: Patrick
Swayze, Charlie Sheen, Lea Thompson. Writer-director Milius
(*The Wind and the Lion*) depicts the heroic exploits of a group of
high school students who resist the Cuban-Soviet takeover of a
small American town sometime in the future.

The Soviet Story (2008). Documentary. 85 minutes. Director: Edvins
Snore. English with subtitles available in fifteen languages. This

is the rarely told story of how the Soviet Union helped Nazi Germany start World War II, initiate the Holocaust, and slaughter its own people on an unprecedented scale. Included are interviews with experts on Soviet terror, the Ukrainian famine of 1932–1933, the Hitler-Stalin Pact of 1939, and the Soviet legacy. Winner of four film festival awards.

PRESIDENTIAL LIBRARIES, OTHER GOVERNMENT WEBSITES, AND UNIVERSITY CENTERS

Cold War International History Project (CWIHP), Woodrow Wilson International Center for Scholars, wilsoncenter.org

Dwight D. Eisenhower Presidential Library, Museum and Boyhood Home, eisenhower.archives.gov

George Bush Presidential Library and Museum, bush41library.tamu. edu

Gerald R. Ford Library & Museum, fordlibrarymuseum.gov

Harry S. Truman Library & Museum, trumanlibrary.org

Harvard University Cold War Studies, projects.iq.harvard.edu

Hoover Institution, Stanford University, hoover.org

Jimmy Carter Presidential Library and Museum, jimmycarterlibrary. gov

John F. Kennedy Presidential Library, jfklibrary.org

LBJ Presidential Library, lbjlibrary.org

Miller Center of Public Affairs, University of Virginia, millercenter. org

National Archives and Records Administration (NARA), archives. gov

Nixon Presidential Library & Museum, nixonlibrary.gov

Ronald Reagan Presidential Foundation & Library, reaganfoundation. org

U.S. Department of State, Office of the Historian, history.state.gov

Victims of Communism Memorial Foundation, victimsofcommunism. org

Yale University Law School Avalon Project, The Cold War, avalon. law.yale.edu

NOTES

ONE: THE ORIGINS OF THE COLD WAR (1917–1945)

1. Alexis de Tocqueville, *Democracy in America*, trans. Harvey C. Mansfield (Chicago: University of Chicago Press, 2000), 395–96.
2. Karl Marx and Friedrich Engels, *The Communist Manifesto*, trans. Samuel Moore (New York: Washington Square Press, 1964), 82.
3. Ibid., 93.
4. Karl Marx and Friedrich Engels, "Manifesto of the Communist Party," in *Marx-Engels Reader*, Robert C. Tucker, ed. (New York: W. W. Norton and Co., 1978), 484, 490.
5. Richard Pipes, *Communism: A History* (New York: Modern Library, 2001), 10–15.
6. V. I. Lenin, "Speech at a Joint Plenum of the Moscow Soviet of Workers, Peasants and Red Army Deputies. Dedicated to the Third Anniversary of the October Revolution, November 6, 1920," *Collected Works*, vol. 31. (Moscow: Progress Publishers, 1974), 397–402.

7. Ibid., 499.
8. Richard Pipes, "The Cold War: CNN's Version," *CNN's Cold War Documentary: Issues and Controversy* (Stanford, Calif.: Hoover Institution Press, 2000), 46.
9. See Harvey Klehr, John Earl Haynes, and Fridrikh Igorevich Firsov, *The Secret World of American Communism* (New Haven, Conn.: Yale University Press, 1995), 8.
10. Brian Crozier, *The Rise and Fall of the Soviet Empire* (Rocklin, CA: Forum, 1999), 62.
11. Ibid., 65.
12. Samuel Eliot Morison, *The Oxford History of the American People*, vol. 3 (New York: New American Library, 1972), 349.
13. Sam Tanenhaus, *Whittaker Chambers: A Biography* (New York: Random House, 1997), 162–63.
14. Crozier, 71.
15. Michael Kort, *The Columbia Guide to the Cold War* (New York: Columbia University Press, 1998), 18.
16. Paul Johnson, *Modern Times: The World from the Twenties to the Eighties* (New York: Harper & Row, 1983), 435.
17. Terry Anderson, *The United States, Great Britain and the Cold War: 1944–1947* (New York: Columbia University Press, 1981), 50.
18. Francis L. Loewenheim, Harold D. Langley, and Manfred Jonas, eds., *From Roosevelt and Churchill: Their Secret Wartime Correspondence* (New York: Saturday Review Press/E. P. Dutton & Co., 1975), Doc. 548, April 11, 1945, p. 709.
19. Walter H. Judd, Report on the War of Ideas in Europe and Asia, *Congressional Record*, pp. A4555–4562.
20. Albert C. Wedemeyer, *Wedemeyer Reports!* (New York: Henry Holt & Company, 1958), 311–12.
21. Walter H. Judd, *Congressional Record*, August 18, 1949, pp. 11787–88.

TWO: CONTAINMENT AND THE SOVIET EXPANSION (1945–1950)

1. For full text of the Long Telegram, see George F. Kennan, *Memoirs: 1925–1950* (Little Brown and Company, 1967), Annex C, 547–59.

2. Elizabeth Edwards Spalding, *The First Cold Warrior: Harry Truman, Containment, and the Remaking of Liberal Internationalism* (Lexington: University Press of Kentucky, 2006), 25.

3. Ibid., 26.

4. Ibid., 30.

5. Lee Edwards, *Congress and the Origins of the Cold War: 1946–1948* (Ann Arbor, Mich.: University Microfilms International, 1986), 6.

6. Ibid.

7. Robert J. Donovan, *Conflict and Crisis: The Presidency of Harry S. Truman, 1945–1948* (New York: W. W. Norton & Company, 1977), 190–91.

8. Address of Winston Churchill, March 5, 1946, Westminster College, Fulton, Missouri, *Congressional Record*, March 6, 1946: House of Representatives: A1145 ff.

9. Ibid.

10. See Spalding, *The First Cold Warrior*, 37–43, for an analysis of the Churchill speech and the reaction in the United States and abroad.

11. *Time*, March 25, 1946, p. 26.

12. "What Does Russia Want?" *New York Times*, editorial, March 14, 1946.

13. Kennan, *Memoirs: 1925–1950*, 547–59.

14. For an extended analysis of the Long Telegram and George Kennan, see John Lewis Gaddis, *Strategies of Containment: A Critical Appraisal of American National Security Policy During the Cold War*, revised edition (New York: Oxford University Press, 2005), 3–21.

15. Memorandum printed in its entirety in *Arthur Krock, Memoirs: Sixty Years on the Firing Line* (New York: Funk and Wagnalls, 1968), 419–82.

16. See Spalding, *The First Cold Warrior*, 53–60, for an examination of the Clifford memorandum.

17. Harry S. Truman, *Memoirs, Volume Two, Years of Trial and Hope* (Garden City, NY: Doubleday & Company, 1956), 99–101.

18. Edwards, *Congress and the Origins of the Cold War*, 44–45.

19. Ibid., 45.

20. Joseph M. Jones, *The Fifteen Weeks* (New York: Viking Press, 1955), 198.

21. See Spalding, 68–71, for a discussion of the Truman Doctrine.

22. George M. Kennan, *Memoirs: 1925–1950*, 354–67. Kennan remarks that the "most serious" deficiency of the article was to state clearly that the "containment" of Soviet power was not the containment by military means of a military threat, but the "political containment of a political threat." This comment directly contradicts the unequivocal call of "X" for a "firm containment designed to confront the Russians with unalterable counter-force at every point where they show signs of encroaching upon the interests of a peaceful and stable world."

23. Spalding, 86.

24. Spalding, 97.

25. Walter Millis, ed., *The Forrestal Diaries* (New York: Viking Press, 1951), 382.

26. Edwards, *Congress and the Origins of the Cold War*, 203.

27. Truman, *Years of Trial and Hope*, 130–31.

28. Carole K. Fink, *Cold War: An International History*, (Boulder, CO: Westview Press, 2014), 72.

29. Spalding, 142–43.

30. Memorandum of Conversation, White House, April 3, 1949, Alonzo L. Hamby, *Man of the People: A Life of Harry S. Truman* (New York: Oxford University Press, 1995), 524.

31. Ibid.

32. Arthur Vandenberg Jr., ed., *The Private Papers of Senator Vandenberg*, (Boston: Houghton Mifflin Company, 1952), 531.
33. John K. Fairbank, *The Great Chinese Revolution, 1800–1985*, (New York: Harper & Row, 1986), 269.
34. Spalding, 181.
35. Martin Malia, *The Soviet Tragedy: A History of Socialism in Russia, 1917–1991* (New York: The Free Press, 1994), 16.
36. As quoted in ibid., 357.
37. See Spalding, 182 ff. for an analysis of NSC 68.
38. Ibid., 187.
39. Ibid., 190.

THREE: THE HOT WARS OF THE COLD WAR (1950–1973)

1. Dean Acheson, *Present at the Creation: My Years in the State Department* (New York: W. W. Norton & Co., 1969), 357.
2. Norman Friedman, *The Fifty-Year War: Conflict and Strategy in the Cold War* (Annapolis, MD: Naval Institute Press, 2000), 152–53.
3. See Brian Crozier, *The Rise and Fall of the Soviet Empire* (Rocklin, CA: Forum, 1999), 150–52; also Appendix E, 579–91.
4. William Chafe, *The Unfinished Journey: America Since World War II* (New York: Oxford University Press, 1995), 249.
5. Samuel Eliot Morison, *The Oxford History of the American People*, vol. 3 (New York: New American Library, 1972), 433–34.
6. Harry Truman, "Address before the Midcentury White House Conference on Children and Youth," December 5, 1950, President Truman's Public Papers, vol. 6, 733–37.
7. Friedman, 167.
8. "The Chance for Peace" Address Delivered Before the American Society of Newspaper Editors, April 16, 1953. Online from Eisenhower.archives.gov; accessed 12/22/15.
9. Diary entry of January 10, 1956, in Robert H. Ferrell, ed., *The Eisenhower Diaries* (New York: W.W. Norton & Company, 1981), 305.

10. Cited in James A. Nathan and Jakes K. Oliver, *United States Foreign Policy and World Order*, 2nd ed. (Boston: Little, Brown and Company, 1981), 176.

11. Ibid, 178

12. James Jay Carafano and Paul Rosenzweig, *Winning the Long War* (Washington, D.C.: Heritage Books, 2005), 9–10.

13. See, for example, Eisenhower to Churchill, February 18, 1955, in Peter G. Boyle, ed., *The Churchill-Eisenhower Correspondence, 1953–1955* (Chapel Hill: The University of North Carolina Press, 1990), 195–98.

14. John Lewis Gaddis, *Strategies of Containment: A Critical Appraisal of Postwar American National Security Policy* (Oxford: Oxford University Press, 1982), 152.

15. The Baghdad Pact, also known as the Middle East Treaty Organization (METO), was renamed the Central Treaty Organization (CENTO) in 1959 after Iraq pulled out of the Pact.

16. Inaugural Address of Dwight D. Eisenhower, delivered at the Capitol, Washington, D.C., January 20, 1953, 83rd Congress, 1st Session, Washington, D.C.: U.S. Government Printing Office, 1953, 2, 4. Online from Eisenhower.archives.gov; accessed 12/22/15.

17. Eisenhower quoted in Gaddis, *Strategies of Containment*, 1982 ed., 136.

18. Ibid., 161.

19. Richard Gid Powers, *Not Without Honor: The History of American Anticommunism* (New York: Free Press, 1995), 260.

20. George Nash, *The Conservative Intellectual Movement in America Since 1945* (New York: Basic Books, 1976), 114–15.

21. George M. Kennan, *Memoirs: 1950–1963* (Boston: Little Brown and Company, 1972), 191–92.

22. Willard Edwards, "McCarthy's Record," *Chicago Tribune*, November 7, 1954.

23. Harvey Klehr, John Earl Haynes, and Fridrikh Igorevich Firsov, *The Secret World of American Communism*, (New Haven: Yale University Press, 1995), 16.

24. Lee Edwards, *Missionary for Freedom: The Life and Times of Walter Judd* (New York: Paragon House, 1990), 221–22.

25. Anne Applebaum, *Iron Curtain: The Crushing of Eastern Europe 1946–1956* (New York: Doubleday, 2012), 457 ff.

26. Ibid.; Stephane Courtois, Nicolas Werth, Jean-Louis Panne, Andrezej Paczkowski, Karel Bartosek, Jean-Louis Margolin, *The Black Book of Communism: Crimes, Terror, Repression*, translated by Jonathan Murphy and Mark Kramer (Cambridge: Harvard University Press, 1999), 439–40.

27. Khrushchev cited in John Lewis Gaddis, *The Cold War: A New History* (New York: The Penguin Press, 2005), 109.

28. Friedman: 214–15.

29. Martin Malia, *The Soviet Tragedy: A History of Socialism in Russia, 1917–1991* (New York: The Free Press, 1994), 13.

30. Friedman, 243.

31. Edwards, *Missionary for Freedom*, 241–42.

32. John F. Kennedy, Inaugural Address, January 20, 1961, Washington, D.C. Online from jfklibrary.org; accessed 12/22/15.

33. Cited in Chafe, *Unfinished Journey*, 187.

34. Gaddis, *The Cold War*, 208.

35. Kennedy, Berlin Speech, June 26, 1963, transcript online from millerrcenter.org; accessed 12/22/15.

36. Crozier, *The Rise and Fall of the Soviet Empire*, 174–77.

37. Katherine A. S. Sibley, *The Cold War* (Westport, CT: Greenwood Press, 1998), 69–70.

38. Paul Johnson, *A History of the American People* (New York: HarperCollins, 1997), 879.

39. Gaddis, *The Cold War*, 235.

40. Cited in Lee Edwards, *Goldwater: The Man Who Made a Revolution*, 2nd ed. (Washington, D.C.: Regnery History, 2015), 311.

41. Johnson, op. cit., 880.

42. Chafe, *Unfinished Journey*, 283.

43. Gaddis, *The Cold War*, 263.

44. See David Halberstam, *The Powers That Be* (New York: Alfred A. Knopf, 1979), 514.

FOUR: DÉTENTE (1969–1980)

1.   David Halberstam, *The Powers That Be* (New York: Alfred A. Knopf, 1979), 268.

2.   For a first-person account of this horrific punishment, see *To Build a Castle: My Life as a Dissenter* by Vladimir Bukovsky (New York: Viking, 1979), who spent twelve years in Soviet prisons, labor camps, and psychiatric hospitals.

3.   As excerpted in Paul Hollander, ed., *From the Gulag to the Killing Fields* (Wilmington, DE: ISI Books, 2006), 41–42.

4.   Norman Friedman, *The Fifty-Year War: Conflict and Strategy in the Cold War* (Annapolis, MD: Naval Institute Press, 2000), 347.

5.   See John Lewis Gaddis, *Russia, the Soviet Union and the United States: An Interpretive History*, 2nd ed., (New York: McGraw-Hill, 1990), 283–84.

6.   Report at a gala joint meeting of the CPSU Central Committee, the Supreme Soviet, and the RSFSR Supreme Soviet, December 21, 1972, quoted in Melvyn Leffler, *For the Soul of Mankind* (New York: Hill and Wang, 2007), 243.

7.   Robert Conquest, *Reflections on a Ravaged Century* (New York: W. W. Norton & Co., 2000), 169.

8.   Henry M. Jackson address to the Fifth International Conference, co-sponsored by the Foundation for Foreign Affairs, Chicago, and the Studien Gesellschaft fur Fragen Mittel und Osteur opaischerr Partnerschaft of Wiesbaden, Chicago, March 23, 1968, in Dorothy Fosdick, ed., *Henry M. Jackson and World Affairs: Selected Speeches, 1953–1983* (Seattle: University of Washington Press, 1990), 103.

9.   Cited in Robert G. Kaufman, *Henry M. Jackson: A Life in Politics* (Seattle: University of Washington Press, 2000), 48.

10. John Lewis Gaddis, *Strategies of Containment: A Critical Appraisal of Postwar American National Security Policy*, 1982 ed. (New York: Oxford University Press, 1982), 280–83.

11. Ibid, 298.

12. The Public Papers of President Richard Nixon 1974, Remarks at Commencement Ceremonies at the U.S. Naval Academy, Annapolis, Maryland, June 5, 1974.

13. Paul Hollander, ed., *From the Gulag to the Killing Fields*, 402.

14. Stephane Courtois, Nicolas Werth, Jean-Louis Panne, Andrzej Paczkowski, Karel Bartosek, Jean-Louis Margolin, *The Black Book of Communism* (Cambridge, MA: Harvard University Press, 1999), 521.

15. Adam B. Ulam, *The Communists: The Story of Power and Lost Illusions 1948-1991* (New York: Charles Scribner's Sons, 1992), 270.

16. Johnson, 908.

17. Hollander, 402.

18. Paul Johnson, *Modern Times: The World from the Twenties to the Eighties* (New York: Harper & Row, 1983), 655.

19. Cited in Gaddis, *The Cold War*, 190–91.

20. For details of Soviet imperialism in the 1970s, see Friedman (pages 400–4, 430–31) and Crozier (pages 233–35, 252–53, 255–56, 349–54).

21. See pages 309–44 of Gaddis's *Strategies of Containment*, 1982 ed., for a comprehensive analysis of the flaws and failures of détente.

22. Jimmy Carter, Inaugural Address, January 20, 1977, and University of Notre Dame Address at Commencement Exercises of the University, May 22, 1977, Public Papers of Jimmy Carter.

23. Lee Edwards, *Missionary for Freedom: The Life and Times of Walter Judd* (New York: Paragon House, 1990), 308–9.

24. For an analysis of *Goldwater v. Carter* and attendant issues, see Lee Edwards, *Goldwater: the Man Who Made a Revolution*, 2nd ed. (Washington: Regnery History, 2015), 418–23.

25. Jimmy Carter, Notre Dame Address.

26. Friedman, 428.

27. Michael Kort, *The Columbia Guide to the Cold War* (New York: Columbia University Press, 1998), 73–74.

28. Jeane J. Kirkpatrick, *Dictatorships and Double Standards*: *Rationalism and Reason in Politics* (New York: AEI/Simon and Schuster, 1982), 49.
29. Ibid.
30. Friedman, 436.
31. Jimmy Carter, State of the Union Address, January 23, 1980, as excerpted in Edward H. Judge and John W. Langdon, *The Cold War*: *A Global History with Documents*, 2nd ed. (Saddle River, NJ: Prentice Hall, 2011), 425.
32. Gaddis, *Strategies of Containment*, 1982 ed., 346.
33. Kort, 76.

FIVE: WINNING THE COLD WAR (1981–1991)

1. Kiron Skinner, Annelise Anderson, and Martin Anderson, eds., *Reagan in His Own Hand*: *The Writings of Ronald Reagan that Reveal His Revolutionary Vision for America* (New York: The Free Press, 2001), 175.
2. Edwards, *The Essential Ronald Reagan* (Lanham, MD: Rowman & Littlefield, 2005), 107.
3. Peter Schweizer, *Victory*: *The Reagan Administration's Secret Strategy That Hastened the Collapse of the Soviet Union* (New York: Atlantic Monthly Press, 1994), xiv.
4. Ibid.
5. John Lewis Gaddis, *The Cold War: A New History* (New York: The Penguin Press, 2005), 217.
6. Rarely in peacetime, writes Hoover Institution Fellow Peter Schweizer, had any president sustained "such a pace of involvement in national security affairs." Peter Schweizer, *Reagan's War* (New York: Doubleday, 2002), 143.
7. Ronald Reagan, "Address to the Nation on Defense and National Security," March 23, 1983. Online by Gerhard Peters and John T. Woolley, The American Presidency Project. http://www.presidency.uscb.edu/ws/?pid=41093.
8. Schweizer, 141.

9. Lou Cannon, *President Reagan: The Role of a Lifetime* (New York: Public Affairs, 2000), 273.

10. Edwards, *The Essential Ronald Reagan*, op. cit., 116.

11. Caspar W. Weinberger, *Fighting for Peace* (New York: Warner Books, 1990), 293–294.

12. Daniel O. Graham, *Confessions of a Cold Warrior* (Fairfax, Va.: Preview Press, 1995), 153.

13. Ronald Reagan, *An American Life* (New York: Simon and Schuster, 1990), 513.

14. Ronald Reagan, "An Address to the Nation," March 4, 1987, Presidential Papers.

15. Edwin Meese III, *With Reagan* (Washington: Regnery Publishing, 1992), 286.

16. Select Committee of the House and Senate, "Report of the Congressional Committees Investigating the Iran-Contra Affair," Washington, D.C.: Government Printing Office, 1987, 437–38.

17. Stephen Sestnovich, "Did the West Undo the East?" in *The Strange Death of Soviet Communism*, edited by Nikolas K. Gvosdev (New Brunswick, N.J.: Transaction, 2008): 35; Crozier, *The Rise and Fall of the Soviet Empire*, 405; Gorbachev's Meeting with Representatives of the French Public, September 29, 1987, FBIS, September 30, 1987: 35, quoted in Leffler, *For the Soul in Mankind*, 414; Friedman, 470.

18. Robert Conquest, *Reflections on a Ravaged Century* (New York: W. W. Norton & Co., 2000), 189.

19. Gaddis, *The Cold War*, 231–32.

20. For the details of the Brandenburg Gate speech, see Ronald Reagan, *An American Life* (New York: Simon & Schuster, 1990), 680–83. Also Peter Robinson, *How Ronald Reagan Changed My Life* (New York: ReganBooks, 2003).

21. Alexis de Tocqueville, *The Old Regime and the Revolution* (New York: Doubleday Anchor Books, 1955), 214.

22. Edwards, *The Essential Ronald Reagan*, 120.

23. Adam B. Ulam, *The Communists: The Story of Power and Lost Illusions 1948–1991* (New York: Charles Scribner's Sons, 1992), 381.

24. Bernard Gwertzman and Michael T. Kaufman, eds., *The Collapse of Communism* (New York: Times Books, 1990), 16.
25. Ivo Banc, ed., *Eastern Europe in Revolution* (Ithaca: Cornell University Press, 1992), 3.
26. George Bush and Brent Scowcroft, *A World Transformed* (New York: Vintage Books, 2011), xvii, 13–14.
27. Carole K. Fink, *Cold War: An International History* (Boulder, CO: Westview Press, 2014), 235–36.
28. Ibid., 236 ff.
29. Bush and Scowcroft, 40–41, 55–56.
30. Don Oberdorfer, *From the Cold War to a New Era: The United States and the Soviet Union, 1983–1991*, new ed. (Baltimore: Johns Hopkins University Press, 1998), 355.
31. Bush and Scowcroft, 149.
32. Ibid., 181.
33. See Fink, *Cold War*, 243–47, for an admirably succinct summary of Germany's reunification.
34. Bush and Scowcroft, 299.
35. Edward H. Judge and John W. Langdon, *The Cold War: A Global History with Documents*, 2nd ed. (Saddle River, NJ: Prentice Hall, 2011), 262.
36. Bush and Scowcroft, 500, 502.
37. Ibid., 515.
38. Michael R. Beschloss and Strobe Talbott, *At the Highest Levels: The Inside Story of the End of the Cold War* (Boston: Little, Brown, 1993), 417–18.
39. Bush and Scowcroft, 516.
40. Judge and Langdon, *The Cold War*, 268; George H. W. Bush, *All the Best, George Bush: My Life in Letters and Other Writings* (New York: Scribner, 2013), 507–9.
41. Gaddis, *The Cold War*, 254.
42. Cited in Lee Edwards, *Mediapolitik: How the Mass Media Transformed World Politics* (Washington: Catholic University Press, 2001), 165.
43. James A. Baker III, *The Politics of Diplomacy: Revolution, War & Peace, 1989–1992* (New York: G. P. Putnam's Sons, 1995), 523.

44. Gaddis, *The Cold War*, 252.
45. William H. Chafe, *The Unfinished Journey: America since World War II* (New York: Oxford University Press, 1995), 501.
46. Bush and Scowcroft, 540.
47. Baker, 563–64.
48. From the transcript of Mikhail S. Gorbachev's resignation speech as recorded through the facilities of CNN and translated by CNN from the Rusian. Reprinted in the *New York Times*, December 26, 1001, A12.
49. Ulam, *The Communists*, 494.
50. Martin Malia, *Russia under Western Eyes: From the Bronze Horseman to the Lenin Mausoleum* (Cambridge: Harvard University Press, 1999), 388.
51. Judge and Langdon, *The Cold War*, 275.
52. Banc, ed., *Eastern Europe in Revolution*, 257.
53. Michael Kort, *The Columbia Guide to the Cold War* (New York: Columbia University Press, 1998), 87–88.
54. Ibid., 88–89.
55. Paul Johnson, *A History of the American People* (New York: HarperCollins, 1997), 930.
56. Fink, *Cold War*, 260.
57. Reagan, *An American Life*, 707–8.
58. John Lewis Gaddis, *Strategies of Containment: A Critical Appraisal of Postwar American National Security Policy*, 2005 ed. (New York: Oxford University Press, 1982), 377.
59. Lech Wałęsa, "Remembering Reagan," *Wall Street Journal*, June 4, 2005.

CONCLUSION: LESSONS FROM THE COLD WAR

1. John Lewis Gaddis, *The Cold War: A New History* (New York: The Penguin Press, 2005), 234.
2. Boris Yeltsin, Address to Joint Session of the U.S. Congress, June 17, 1992.

INDEX

A

Acheson, Dean, 39–40, 54, 66–67
Africa, 1, 87, 94, 99, 101, 112, 178
"Agreement on Ending the War
    and Restoring Peace in Viet-
    nam, An," 119
Albania, 202, 208
Aleutians, the, 66
Allen, Richard, 147
American Communist Party, the,
    79, 81
"American Relations with the
    Soviet Union," 36–37
Amin, Hafizulah, 139
Andropov, Yuri, 151, 153, 156,
    220–21
Angola, 112, 125–26, 129, 141,
    149, 217, 221

anti-ballistic missile system, 151
Anti-Ballistic Missile Treaty (ABM
    Treaty), 216
Armenia, 8
armistice talks, 69–70, 207
Army-McCarthy hearings, 79
Asia, 1, 8–9, 22, 54–55, 75, 94,
    99–100, 102–3, 112, 118, 127,
    178, 198
Atlantic alliance, the, 53, 141
Atlee, Clement, 26, 202
Australia, 75, 208
Austria, 18, 83, 166, 202, 222
Azerbaijan, 8, 32

B

Baghdad Pact, the, 75, 208
Baker, James, 171, 184

balance-of-power politics, 35
Baltic states, 8, 12, 27, 171, 180
Bamboo Curtain, the, 56–58, 72,
    100, 126, 133
"Basic Principles" statement, 127
Bay of Pigs, 95, 212
BBC, the, 187
Begin, Menachem, 138
Beijing, 112, 118, 129, 168–69, 196
Belgium, 52, 153
Berle, A. A., 14
Berlin, 50–51, 61, 91, 95–96, 173,
    175, 210, 212–13, 221
    Berlin Airlift, the, 50–51, 61,
        195
    Berlin blockade, the, 44, 50, 205
    Berlin Wall, the, 96–97, 161,
        164, 167, 174–75, 196, 212,
        221, 223
    East Berlin, 96, 207, 212
    West Berlin, 50–51, 96, 167, 212
Bern meeting, 19
B-52s, 99
Bill of Rights, the, 60
"Black Berets," 180–81
Black Book of Communism, 83
Black Sea, the, 26, 28, 32, 202–3
Bolshevik Revolution, 6, 156, 184,
    201
Bolsheviks, the, 7–8, 201
Brandenburg Gate, 161, 221
Brezhnev, Leonid, 107–11, 123–
    24, 127, 135, 141, 151, 153,
    197, 213, 218, 220
Brezhnev Doctrine, the, 110, 152,
    167, 171, 173, 194, 222
British, the, 16–17, 26, 31, 96,
    121, 142, 204

British Embassy, 38
British Parliament, the, 146, 220
Brzezinski, Zbigniew, 135
Buckley, William F., Jr., 77
Budapest, 82, 166–67, 223
Bukovsky, Vladimir, 108
Bulgaria, 18, 41, 44, 202, 208
Bush, George Herbert Walker,
    169–84, 195–96, 222
Bush-Gorbachev summit, 177–78,
    181
Byelorussia, 8, 13, 18

C
Cambodia, 100, 112, 117, 120–
    22, 138, 149, 215, 217, 221
Camp David Accords, the, 138
Canada, 52
Carafano, James Jay, 73
Carter, Jimmy, 111, 125, 128,
    130–40, 149, 161, 198, 218–19
Carter Doctrine, the, 140, 219
Casey, William, 147, 155
Castro, Fidel, 88–89, 95, 99, 110,
    209–12
Caucasus, the, 8
Ceausescu, Nicolae, 167, 223
CENTO, 208. *See also* Baghdad
    Pact, the
Chafe, William H., 183
Chambers, Whittaker, 12, 14, 77,
    205
Charter of Paris for a New
    Europe, the, 224
Charter of the United Nations,
    the, 67
Charter 77 group, 125, 157, 217
Cheney, Dick, 171
Chernenko, Konstantin, 153, 221

Chile, 10, 129

China, 2, 9, 20–22, 26, 28, 54–59, 68–69, 72, 75, 77, 80, 86, 100, 103, 112, 115, 117–19, 121–22, 126–27, 129, 131, 167–69, 193, 196, 199, 208, 210, 212–13, 223. *See also* People's Republic of China (PRC), the Nationalist China, Nationalist Chinese, 20–22, 54–55, 74, 206

Christian Democrats, 12

Churchill, Winston, 16–20, 25–26, 30–32, 37, 47, 202–3

CIA, the, 88, 90, 95, 147, 150, 155, 169, 204, 212

Clark, William P., 147

Clayton, Will, 47

Clifford, Clark, 36–37

CNN, 182, 185

Columbia University, 70

Comintern, the. *See* Communist International, the

Common Market, the, 210

communism, 2–3, 9, 22, 27, 35–37, 46, 48, 57–58, 62, 68, 84, 86, 93, 95, 114, 124, 130, 139–40, 143, 146, 160–61, 164–65, 170, 173–75, 181, 185, 188, 192, 195–96, 203, 220

Communist International, 9

Communist International, the, 9–10, 12, 16, 46

Communist Manifesto, The, 6, 158

Communist Party, the, 56, 79, 81, 85, 107–9, 119, 126, 156, 158, 160, 162–64, 167–68, 181–83,

201, 207, 209, 213, 221, 223–24

Congress of People's Deputies, the, 222

Conquest, Robert, 87

Constitution, the, 60

containment, 23, 27, 35, 42, 44–46, 48, 51–54, 62, 65, 70–76, 92, 113, 125, 127, 140, 149–50, 186–87, 194, 197, 204

Conventional Armed Forces in Europe Treaty, the, 224

Cooper-Church Amendment, 117

Council of Mutual Economic Assistance (Comecon), 59

Crimea, 16, 181, 202

Cronkite, Walter, 105

Crozier, Brian, 13, 97

Cuba, 88–89, 95, 97–99, 125, 129, 136, 187, 209–12, 219

Cuban Missile Crisis, the, 97–99, 212

Curzon Line, the, 18

Czechoslovakia, 16–18, 44, 49–50, 109, 125, 157, 167, 173, 204, 208, 214, 217, 223

Czechoslovak Republic, 49

D

Dardanelles, the, 32

Declaration of Independence, the, 60

"Declaration on Liberated Europe," 19

de Gaulle, Charles, 47, 101

democracy, 17–18, 24–25, 27, 33, 36–37, 40, 49, 52, 63, 69–70, 87, 96, 130, 143, 145–46, 150, 152, 163, 167, 180–81, 183,

186–88, 192, 195, 198, 204, 220, 223

Democracy in America (Tocqueville), 6

Democratic National Committee headquarters, 216

Democratic People's Republic of Korea, the, 66, 205

Democrats, Democratic Party (U.S.), 3, 24, 54, 65, 93, 102, 113, 130–31, 175, 216

Denmark, 15

deportations, 2, 85, 87

Depression, the, 79

"de-Stalinization," 85–88, 209

détente, 3, 59, 107–40, 145–46, 161, 198
  and Afghanistan, 138–40
  failure of, 123–30
  and Jimmy Carter, 130–38
  and Nixon and Kissinger, 111–23

"Dictatorships and Double Standards," 137

Diem, Ngo Dinh, 213

Dimitrov, Georgi, 10

diplomacy, 2–3, 14, 21, 92, 118, 131, 133, 135, 149–50, 169, 176, 193, 198, 203, 211, 218

Distinguished Flying Cross, 169

Dobrynin, Anatoly, 124

domestic affairs, 2–3, 8, 28, 41–43, 56–57, 112–13, 116, 133, 167, 197

Douglas, William O., 29

Dubcek, Alexander, 109

Dulles, John Foster, 47, 72–75, 84, 93

E

Eagleburger, Lawrence, 147

Eastern Europe, 2, 8, 19, 23, 30, 40, 59, 83–84, 112, 128, 148, 165, 168–69, 173, 175, 177, 192, 194, 197, 202, 218, 222

Egypt, 84, 123, 125, 138, 209

Eisenhower, Dwight D., 65, 70–76, 78, 80–85, 88–94, 100, 103, 114–15, 207, 209–10

Eisenhower Doctrine, 74, 210

El Salvador, 149

Elsey, George M., 36–37

Enlai, Zhou, 118

Estonia, 8, 10, 12, 174, 223

Ethiopia, 125, 157, 216

European Recovery Program (ERP), 48–49, 204, 207

"evil empire," 3, 150, 161, 194

F

Fairbank, John K., 55

famines, forced famines, 2, 11, 57, 86, 122, 164

Federal Republic of Germany, the, 153, 205

Fifth Amendment, the (U.S. Constitution), 78

Fink, Carole K., 51, 187

Finland, 9, 12

Firsov, Fridrikh Igorevich, 81

forced relocation, 11

Ford, Gerald, 111, 121, 125, 127, 130, 216

foreign affairs, 2, 28, 41, 97, 113, 137

Foreign Affairs (journal), 44, 46, 204

Formosa, island of, 206. *See also* Taiwan
Forrestal, James, 36, 49
Fort Worth, Texas, 101
Four Old-Fashioned Things, the, 118
"Four Policemen," the, 26
France, 9, 15–16, 18, 24, 44, 46–47, 52, 84–85, 90, 176, 208–9
Franklin D. Roosevelt (the aircraft carrier), 33
freedom, 2, 6, 14, 24, 39, 43, 51–52, 60, 63, 68, 75, 82–83, 86, 88, 93, 96, 101, 115, 142–44, 146–47, 149–50, 161–64, 171, 179, 183, 187–88, 195, 198, 209, 222
   economic freedom, 2, 144
   religious freedom, 14, 143
Free French, the, 47
Friedman, Norman, 104
Fuchs, Klaus, 77
Fulton, Missouri, 203

G

Gaddis, John Lewis, 125, 146, 161
Galbraith, John Kenneth, 145
"Gang of Eight," 181–82, 224
Gareev, Makhmut, 151
Geneva, 160, 221
Georgia, 8, 183
German Democratic Republic (East Germany), 59, 91, 167, 175–77, 205, 208, 212, 223,
Germany, 9–12, 16–18, 25, 51, 59, 91, 122, 142, 153, 166–67, 175–77, 202, 205, 208, 212, 215, 223
glasnost, 159–63, 170, 192

Goldwater, Barry, 132–33
Gorbachev, Mikhail, 146, 152, 156–64, 167–74, 177, 177–88, 192, 194, 196, 221, 222, 224
Gorki, 219, 160
Gottwalk, Klement, 49
Great Britain, 2, 9, 15, 18–19, 26–27, 38–39, 52, 75, 85, 90, 153, 193, 202–3, 213, 218
"Great Helmsman," the, 126
Great Leap Forward, the, 57, 168, 210
Great Proletarian Cultural Revolution), 57, 118
"great Satan," the, 136
Great Terror, the, 10–11, 57, 86, 164
Greece, 39–42, 51, 129, 203–4, 207
Greek and Turkish aid bill, 41
Grenada, 152, 220
Guatemala, 74
Gulag, the, 11, 57, 87, 108, 212, 218
Gulag Archipelago, The (Solzhenitzyn), 58, 216
Gulf of Tonkin Resolution, the, 103, 117, 213
Guzman, Jacobo Arbenz, 74

H

Hanoi, 119, 121
Harriman, Averell, 19, 26
Harvard University, 44, 48, 55, 145, 148
Havel, Václav, 125, 166–67, 173, 194, 217, 222–23
Hawaii, 54

Haynes, John Earl, 81
Helsinki Accords, the, 123–25, 187, 217
Hero Square, 82
Herter, Christian, 90
Hiss, Alger, 14, 77, 79, 113, 205
Hitler, Adolf, 11–12, 15–16, 31, 98, 233
Ho Chi Minh City, 121
Hollander, Paul, 118
Holodomor, the, 11, 57
Honecker, Erich, 167, 196
Hook, Steven. W., 186
House Un-American Activities Committee, the, 113
Hudson Bay, the, 98
Hue, Vietnam, 104
Hungarian freedom fighters, 83
Hungarian Revolution of 1956, the, 83–84, 194, 209, 223
Hungary, 9, 16, 18, 41, 81–84, 86, 173, 174, 205, 208, 222
hydrogen bomb, the, 59, 206

I

"Ich bin ein Berliner" speech, the, 213
Indochina War, the, 22, 204, 215
INF Treaty, the, 196, 222
intercontinental ballistic missiles, 88, 107, 160
  1054 American ICBMs, 128
  1330 Soviet ICMBs, 128
International Monetary Fund, the, 33
Iran, 9, 27, 32, 59, 75, 129, 136–37, 153–56, 193, 198, 203, 208, 219–21

Iran-Contra scandal, the, 153–56, 221
Iran hostage crises, the, 136–37, 153–55, 219–20
Iraq, 75, 208
Iron Curtain, 29–30, 32, 39, 56, 62, 83, 165–66, 173, 186, 188, 194, 203
Iron Curtain speech, 30, 32, 203
Italy, 10, 44, 46, 153

J

Jackson, Henry, 113
Japan, Japanese, 16–17, 20–21, 25, 28, 66, 68, 74, 115, 202
Jessup, Philip, 54
John Paul II (pope), 143, 194, 218. *See also* Wojtyła, Karol
Johnson, Lyndon B., 55, 101–3, 105, 107, 117, 213
Johnson, Paul, 121–22, 187
Joint Chiefs of Staff, 70, 204
Judd, Walter, 22, 55, 81, 13
Judge, Edward, 185

K

Kai-shek, Chiang, 20–21, 54–55
Kansas, 71
Katyn Forest massacre, 13, 164
Kazakhstan, 8
Kennan, George, 23–24, 33–37, 44–46, 52, 58, 75, 79, 149, 203–4
Kennedy, John F., 65, 89, 91–101, 115, 134, 211–13
Kennedy, Robert, 98
Kent State University, 117, 215
KGB, 13, 87, 108, 162, 181. *See also* NKVD

Khomeini, Ayatollah, 136
Khrushchev, Nikita, 85–87,
    89–92, 94–97, 99, 107, 109,
    197, 207, 209–11, 213
"Killing Fields," the, 122
Kirghizstan, 8
Kirkpatrick, Jeane, 137
Kissinger, Henry, 111, 114–16,
    118, 120, 125–27, 129, 161,
    198
"Kitchen Debate," the, 211
Klehr, Harvey, 81
Kohl, Helmut, 142, 175–76
Korea, Korean, 2, 9, 22, 28, 56,
    66–70, 75, 77, 80, 112, 129,
    131, 138, 187, 193, 202, 205–7,
    214, 220
Korean Air Lines Flight 007, 220
Korean War, the, 22, 56, 66–70,
    80
Kort, Michael, 136–37, 186
Krakow, 143, 218
Krauthammer, Charles, 149
Kremlin, the, 13, 26–27, 34, 36–38,
    41, 45–46, 51, 60, 62, 67, 71,
    81, 92, 109–10, 118, 139, 142,
    147, 152, 161, 185, 194, 213
Kristol, Irving, 77

L

Langdon, John, 185
laogai, the, 57
Laos, 100, 117, 121, 138, 211, 217
Latin America, 1, 75, 94, 97, 99,
    101, 112, 149
Latvia, 8, 12, 174, 180, 223
Lau, Ha Van, 122
Leahy, William D., 18
Lebanon, 74, 153

Leipzig, East Germany, 223
Lend-Lease Act, 15
Lenin, Vladimir, 6–8, 10, 12, 110,
    163–64, 181, 183–84, 196, 201
Leninist Doctrine, the, 110
Lima, Peru, 98
Lippmann, Walter, 47
Lithuania, 8, 12, 174, 180, 223
Litvinov, Maxim, 14
London, 18, 47, 49, 112, 152, 178
"Long Telegram," 23–24, 33,
    35–37, 203
Lovett, Robert, 51
Lublin, 18
Lukhim, Vladimir, 187
Luxembourg, 52

M

MacArthur, Douglas, 68–70, 206
Machiavelli, 192
Malia, Martin, 57, 87, 185
Manchuria, 21–22
Marine Corps, 94
Marshall, George, 39–40, 44, 48,
    54–55, 204
Marshall Plan, the, 24, 44, 46–50,
    52, 63, 193, 198, 204
martial law, 141, 165, 220
Marx, Karl, 6–8, 97
Marxism, 7, 37, 74, 89, 125, 137,
    150, 152, 157, 197–98, 213, 220
Marxism-Leninism, 8, 12, 56, 61,
    87, 121, 141, 146, 165, 177,
    188, 192, 194
Massachusetts, 93
Matsu, 74
Mayaguez, the, 217
McCarthy, Joseph, 76–80, 206,
    208

"McCarthyism," 77
McNamara, Robert, 98, 117
Meese, Edwin, III, 155
Mekong River, 122
Mexico, 126
Middle East, 9, 27, 74–75, 85, 178, 208–10
Mikołajczyk, Stanisław, 41
Mindszenty, Joseph, 82, 205
Minh, Ho Chi, 100, 102, 121
Missouri, 24, 203
Moldavia, 8
Molotov, Vyacheslav, 26
Molotov-Ribbentrop Non-Aggression Pact, 11, 174, 202. *See also* Nazi-Soviet Pact
Monroe Doctrine of 1823, 42, 88, 99
Morison, Samuel Eliot, 13–14
Moscow, 10, 12, 14, 16, 23, 30, 32–33, 36, 41, 60, 66, 86, 88, 90, 96–99, 107, 112, 124, 129, 135, 139, 145, 151, 156, 162–64, 167, 171, 174, 178–82, 187, 196, 203, 211, 218, 222
Moscow State University, 163, 222
Mozambique, 112, 126, 129, 141, 217
Munich, 31, 51, 98
mutual assured destruction (MAD), 151

N

Nagy, Imre, 167, 223
Nasser, Gamal, 84, 209
National Guard, 117
National Security Act, the, 204
National Security Council, 37, 58, 98, 146, 148, 154, 204

Nazis, 12–13, 15, 122, 202
Nazi-Soviet Pact, 202. *See also* Molotov-Ribbentrop Non-Aggression Pact
Netherlands, the, 52, 153
New Deal, the, 102
New Economic Plan, 158
"New Look," the, 71, 74, 76
Newsweek, 29
New York Times, the, 31, 179
New Zealand, 75, 208
Nicaragua, 112, 126, 136–37, 141, 149–50, 153, 155, 157, 198, 219–22
Nitze, Paul, 58, 94
Nixon, Richard, 59, 89, 111, 113–20, 123, 125–27, 129–30, 154–56, 161, 169, 195–96, 198, 211, 215–16
Nixon Doctrine, the, 115, 215
NKVD, 13, 41. *See also* KGB
nomenklatura, the, 162
nonaggression pact between West Germany and the Soviet Union, 215
North, Oliver, 155
North Atlantic Treaty Organization (NATO), 24, 44, 46, 48, 50–54, 63, 70, 74, 91, 134–35, 141–42, 153, 176–78, 193, 205, 207–8, 219–20
Norway, 15, 153
NSC 68, 37, 44, 58–63, 68, 75, 94, 206
NSDD-73, 148–49
NSDD-66, 148
NSDD-32, 148
Nuclear Non-Proliferation Treaty, 215

O

One Day in the Life of Ivan Denisovich, 212
Operation Rolling Thunder, 214
Ortega, Daniel, 150
Oswald, Lee Harvey, 213
Oval Office, the, 174

P

Pakistan, 75, 129, 208
Paris, 41, 49, 90, 119, 122, 152, 216, 224
"peaceful coexistence," 34, 87, 110–12
Pearl Harbor, 15
Pentagon, the, 78, 88, 104, 147, 214
People's Liberation Army, the, 57, 103, 119
People's Republic of China (PRC), the, 21, 56, 59, 69, 131, 138, 206, 215–16, 218. *See also* China
Peress, Irving, 78, 80
perestroika, 158–59, 161–62, 170, 192
Perm Gulag, the, 218
Persia, 9
Persian Gulf, the, 140, 198, 219
Persian Gulf War, the, 178
Philippines, the, 54, 66, 74–75, 129, 208
Pipes, Richard, 7–8, 148
Poindexter, John, 155
Poland, 9, 12–13, 17–18, 26, 44, 86, 91, 141, 143–44, 148, 157, 165–66, 173, 188, 194, 202, 208–9, 218

Polish Peasant Party, 41
Polish Solidarity movement, 166
Politburo, the, 107, 151, 176, 180–81, 224
Portugal, 125, 129
Pot, Pol, 122
Potsdam conference, 25–27, 202
Powers, Francis Gary, 90
Poznan, Poland, 209
"Prague Spring," the, 109, 124, 214
"Preemptive Strike Operations Plan," 67
PT 109, 93
Public Group to Promote Observance of the Helsinki Accords, 124
purges, 2, 11, 87
Pushkin, Alexander, 163

Q

Quemoy, 74, 210

R

Radio Free Europe, 83
Radio Liberty, 187
Reagan, Ronald, 3, 135, 137, 140, 172, 185, 188, 194–95, 219
  "ash-heap of history," 177
  comparison to foreign policy of Bush administration, 177–75
  and end of Cold War, 187–88
  Gorbachev and, 156–163
  Intermediate-Range Nuclear Forces treaty signed by, 178–79
  Iran-Contra "scandal," 153–56

policy of mutual assured
    destruction (MAD), 151–53
strategy of change rather than
    contain Soviet Union, 145–50
winning the Cold War, 141–44
Reagan Doctrine, 188, 193, 198,
    221
Real-politik, 192
Red Army, the, 12, 16, 20, 41, 57,
    194
Red Guards, the, 103, 118–19
Red Square, 163, 183
religion, 2, 8, 36
Republican Eightieth Congress, 49
Republicans, Republican Party,
    39–40, 76, 170
Republic of China, 20–21, 56, 59,
    68–69, 74–75, 118, 127, 131,
    138, 206, 215–16, 218
Republic of Korea, the, 66, 205
Reykjavik, 160, 221
Reykjavik summit, the, 161
Rhee, Syngman, 66
Rice, Condoleezza, 172
Rio Pact, 75
Robinson, Roger, 148
Rogers, William, 119
Romania, 18, 41, 109, 167, 203,
    208, 223
Roosevelt, Franklin (FDR), 14, 19,
    25–26, 102
Rosenberg, Ethel, 77, 207
Rosenberg, Julius, 77, 207
Rosenzweig, Paul, 73
Rouge, Khmer, 121–22, 217
Rusk, Dean, 94, 96, 98
Russia, 2, 5, 7–9, 13, 15, 18, 23,
    27–28, 30, 34, 36–37, 45–46,
    61, 72, 82, 87–88, 99, 113,

124–25, 145, 148, 163, 172,
    174, 176, 181–85, 188, 199,
    201, 203, 219, 224. *See also*
    USSR
Russian Civil War, the, 8, 201
Ryukyu Islands, the, 66

S

Sadat, Anwar, 138
Saigon, 104, 121, 217
Sakharov, Andrei, 124, 160, 219
SALT II, 133, 135, 139, 142, 218
Schlesinger, Arthur, Jr., 145
"scientific socialism," 7
Scowcroft, 170–73, 175, 177, 179
Senate Permanent Subcommittee,
    the, 78
Seoul, 69, 220
Shakespeare, William, 58
Sharansky, Natan, 160, 218
Siberia, 218
Sibley Katherine A. S., 98
Sino-Japanese war, 20
Sino-Soviet split, the, 221
Social Democrats, 12
socialism, 16, 75, 87, 109–10, 126,
    157–58, 173, 183, 186, 192,
    196, 211
Solidarity, 148, 157, 165–67, 194,
    219–20, 223
Solzhenitsyn, Aleksandr, 58, 212
Somalia, 125
Somoza regime, 136
"Sources of Soviet Conduct, The,"
    44, 204
Southeast Asian Treaty Organiza-
    tion (SEATO), the, 208
South Yemen, 125

Soviet Communist Party, the, 81,
207
Soviet expansionism, expansion,
2, 6, 11, 17, 21, 30, 44, 140,
144, 205
Soviet NKVD, 13, 41
Soviet Union, 53–54, 65, 86, 94, 97,
99–100, 139, 130–31, 151–52,
163–66, 196–98, 201, 204–6,
209–10, 213, 215, 219, 221–34
Bamboo Curtain and, 56–58
calls for "wars of national liberation," 112–23
Chinese communists and,
21–22
communist ideology of, 1–3, 6,
10
containment and Soviet expansion, 25–29, 31–38
the Cuban challenge and,
90–92
"democratization" of, 163–66
failure of Nixon's détente,
123–30
George Herbert Walker Bush
as last president of the Cold
War, 169–77
Gorbachev as general secretary
of the Communist Party,
156–63
Hungarian Revolution and
communism in Eastern
Europe, 84–85
Korean War and, 66–70
Leonid Brezhnev replaces
Nikita Khrushchev, 107–11
Marxism-Leninism headed for
Reagan's "ash-heap of history," 177–93

National Security Council
Report 68 and, 58–63
negotiations at Yalta, 16–20
Reagan sees Soviet Union as
greatest threat to free world,
144–50
Senator McCarthy and the ring
of spies, 76–81
"Sources of Soviet Conduct,
44–46
Stalin and the Great Terror,
12–14, 16
Truman Doctrine and, 38–46
Spain, 220
Spanier, John, 187
Sputnik I, 87
SS-20, 128, 141, 193, 218
Stalin, Joseph, 3, 10, 194, 201
State of the Union address, 27
Stettinius, Edward, 25
Strategic Arms Limitations Treaty
(SALT I), the, 110, 128, 133,
216
Strategic Arms Reduction Treaty,
the, 178
Strategic Defense Initiative (SDI),
the, 151, 220
Suez Canal, the, 84, 123, 209
Suez Crisis, the, 74, 84
Sung, Kim Il, 66–67
Sweden, 9
Syria, 123

T

Taiwan, 22, 68, 74, 118–19, 131–
32, 138, 206, 208, 210, 218
Taiwan Relations Act, the, 131,
133
Taiwan Straits, 74, 208, 210

Tajikistan, 8

"tear down this wall" speech, 161, 221

Teheran, 136, 219

Tet offensive of January 1968, the, 104–5, 214

Thailand, 75, 119, 208

Thatcher, Margaret, 142, 194, 218

Third World, the, 110, 125–26, 136, 164, 187

Tho, Le Duc, 119

Tiananmen Square, 168–69, 223

Tiananmen Square Massacre, the, 223

To Build a Castle (Vladimir Bukovsky), 108

Tocqueville, Alexis de, 5

totalitarianism, 2, 41, 195

Totalitarian State, 27, 87

Treaty on German Unity, the, 176

Trotskyites, 12

Truman, Harry, 3, 20–21, 56, 65, 77, 91–94, 100, 113, 115, 143–44, 147, 161, 169, 185, 194–95, 202–6

descent of the Iron Curtain and, 21–33

the Long Telegram, 33–38

the Marshall Plan, 46–50

National Security Council 68(NSC 68), 58–63

NATO, 50–54

policy of containment, 68–72

Truman Doctrine, the, 24, 33, 38–39, 42, 44, 48–49, 52, 63

Tsarist regime, 7

Turkey, 28, 32, 38–42, 51, 75, 99, 203, 204, 207–8, 212

Turkmenistan, 8

Twentieth Party Congress, 85, 107

U

Ukraine, 8, 11, 13, 57, 86, 180, 183

Ulam, Adam, 119, 165, 185

Unification of Germany, 176, 223

Union of Soviet Socialist Republics. *See* USSR

United Kingdom, the, 208

United Nations (UN), 2, 17, 28, 42, 67–68, 70, 89, 112, 137, 169, 171, 202–3, 206, 211

United States, the, 2–3, 6, 8–10, 22–23, 25–28, 50–51, 56, 59–60, 65, 66–68, 83–85, 88–91, 94, 97–101, 105–6, 154, 175–76, 184–88, 198–99, 203–4, 206, 208, 210–13, 215–16, 218 218–21

American Communist Party, 81

Carter Doctrine proclaimed, 132, 135, 137–40

challenge to Soviet imperialism, 39–40, 42, 44

containment as the proper policy toward the Soviet Union, 47

détente and Nixon, 107–123

the failure of détente, 123–130

German occupation zones, 18–19

Gorbachev and the, 157, 161, 171–74,

ideals and principles of, 192–97

isolationist sentiment in the, 13–15

main thesis of the Clifford-Elsey Memorandum, 33–38

the Marshall Plan, 46–48
NATO and the, 74–77
new strategies for winning the
Cold War, 144–53
one of the "Four Policemen," 26
threatens to withdraw support
and trade agreements,
180–81
University of Notre Dame, 130
Uruguay, 126
U.S. Congress, 117, 120–21, 127,
129, 131–33, 150, 155, 169,
204, 209, 217, 220
U.S. Department of Defense, 204
Uskorenye, 158
U.S. Naval Academy, 115, 130
U.S. Pershing II missiles, 142, 153,
221
USS *Pueblo*, the, 214
USSR, 6, 14–15, 25–27, 29, 46,
59, 123, 173–74, 176, 180,
202–3, 206–9, 211–12, 216–
17, 220, 222, 224
basic attitudes of, 34
Bush grants most-favored-
nation trading status to the,
178
debilitated position of Gorbachev in the, 170–71
Kennan's analysis of threat to
democratic countries by the,
36
nuclear imbalance between the
United States and the, 97
official termination of the, 185
the primary weakness of,
62–63
the Reagan Doctrine as a strategy for defeating the, 149,
151

Reagan sought to defeat the,
143
the tyranny of the, 57
U.S. State Department, 14, 22–23,
33, 38, 47, 56, 58, 76, 79, 90,
129, 147, 176, 196, 206
U.S. Supreme Court, 29, 133
Uzbekistan, 8

V

Vance, Cyrus, 134
Vandenberg, Arthur, 40, 55
Vandenberg Resolution, 50
Van Fleet, James, 69
Van Thieu, Nguyen, 121
VC-NVA (Viet-Cong and North
Vietnamese Army), 104
V-E Day, 24, 202
Vienna, 16, 83, 95
Vietnam, 2, 55, 95, 125, 129,
138–39, 157, 193, 196, 298,
208–9, 212–17
historians call war an egregious
blunder caused by containment policy, 186–87
Nixon-Kissinger foreign policy,
116–22
secret negotiations with China
to encourage end of conflict
in, 119–22
"secret plan" of Nixon's to seek
negotiated end to the war
in, 118
struggle for control of, 100–6
U.S. unable to achieve final
military victory over North,
112–14, 16
Vietnam peace agreement
signed in Paris, 119
Vietnamese nationalists, 100, 208

"Vietnamization," 114, 215
Vietnam Peace Agreement, 216
V-J Day, 29, 202
Voice of America, 187

W

Walesa, Lech, 187, 194
War Powers Resolution, 120
Warsaw, 16, 143
Warsaw Pact, the, 109, 164, 194,
    208, 214, 224
Washington, D.C., 14, 23–24, 29,
    33, 35, 38, 48, 52, 88, 98–99,
    105, 112–13, 118, 130, 145,
    177, 203, 216
Watergate scandal, 120, 130,
    154–55, 216
Weinberger, Caspar, 147, 151, 154
Western Europe, 2, 10, 44, 48–49,
    50–52, 54, 113, 128, 142, 153,
    210, 218–19, 221
Westminster College, 30
West Point, 71
Wheeling, West Virginia, 76
White, Harry Dexter, 79
Wojtyła, Karol, 218. *See also* John
    Paul II (pope)
World Bank, the, 33
World War I, 1, 7–9, 24, 49
World War II, 1, 11, 24, 29, 31,
    38, 46–47, 66, 78, 93, 114,
    130–32, 139, 142, 176–77,
    198, 202, 203, 207
    economic consequences in
        Great Britain, 38
    FDR winning of, 102
    George Herbert Walker Bush
        received Distinguished Fly-
        ing Cross during, 169

increased trade with Soviet
    Union post war, 123
invasion of Poland in 1939 trig-
    gered, 165–66
mass deportation of ethnic
    minorities during, 85
Stalin blames war on "monop-
    oly capitalism," 31
"World War III," 29, 59

X

"X," 44, 46, 204

Y

Yalta conference, the, 6, 16–19,
    22, 25–26, 202, 204
Yalu River, the, 69
Yeltsin, Boris, 13, 181–184, 192,
    224
Yom Kippur War, 123

Z

Zablocki, Clement, 132
Zaslavskaya, Tatyana, 159
Zedong, Mao, 20–22, 54, 56, 118,
    206, 217
Zinoviev, Grigorii, 9
Zwicker Ralph W., 78